"I would like to dedicate this book to the memory of my Grandfather,

He was and always will be the greatest chef I knew and

the person who always believed in me,

his memory Lives on through my work everyday"

"Modern Patisserie" is how Sarah describes her work and without doubt, this young chef's work is at the cutting edge of pastry making today. Whilst often playful, fanciful and contemporary in style, Sarah's creative talent is founded on solid training and for over 18 years, Sarah has honed her skills at the very finest establishments including Head Pastry Chef roles at Hakkasan Group's Yauatcha, Dinner By Heston Blummental, ME London and most recently, at the glamorous Corinthia Hotel London. Her previous work, at reputable 5 star hotels Mandarin Oriental, The Ritz and The Connaught, further helped sharpen Sarah's pastry prowess. At the helm of these great city institutions, Sarah is herself a true Londoner, having spent nearly all of her career in the capital and London's dynamism and sophistication has clearly helped shape her work. But perhaps what has inspired Sarah's work the most are childhood memories of her grandfather, himself a professional chef.

Watching him in the kitchen as a child ignited in Sarah a passion for creation and a fierce love of cooking. That same drive and sense of childhood reverie are essential elements seen in Sarah's work today. In "Patisserie Perfection", Sarah's very first Pastry Book, she shares recipes for some of her most fantastical desserts. Spanning 200 recipes, ranging from pralines and petits gâteaux to her beloved deconstructed desserts, this book encapsulates the very essence of Sarah's style: imaginative, daring and always novel. "I don't copy ideas, I like to create. I take inspiration from every day items around me. I like to take small elements, little bits and pieces from things I see and rework them into something new." That innovative spirit is most evident in her recipes, in which she demonstrates a modern twist on classic desserts, and the sheer magic of her entremets, where Sarah says she gets the "opportunity to be most creative, to have fun." There is indeed a joyful whimsy to her work and Sarah Barber is the very personification of her creations: herself as dainty in appearance as her ethereal and exquisite work. Yet the delicacy of her handiwork belies its tough technique. In this colourful compendium, Sarah unravels the mystery of pastry to reveal the secrets behind her artistry. Read it and you may suddenly find yourself transported to a magical land. Try the recipes and you will be inspired to explore your own creativity. Taste them, and you'll be glad you did. This is, after all, patisserie perfected.

SB

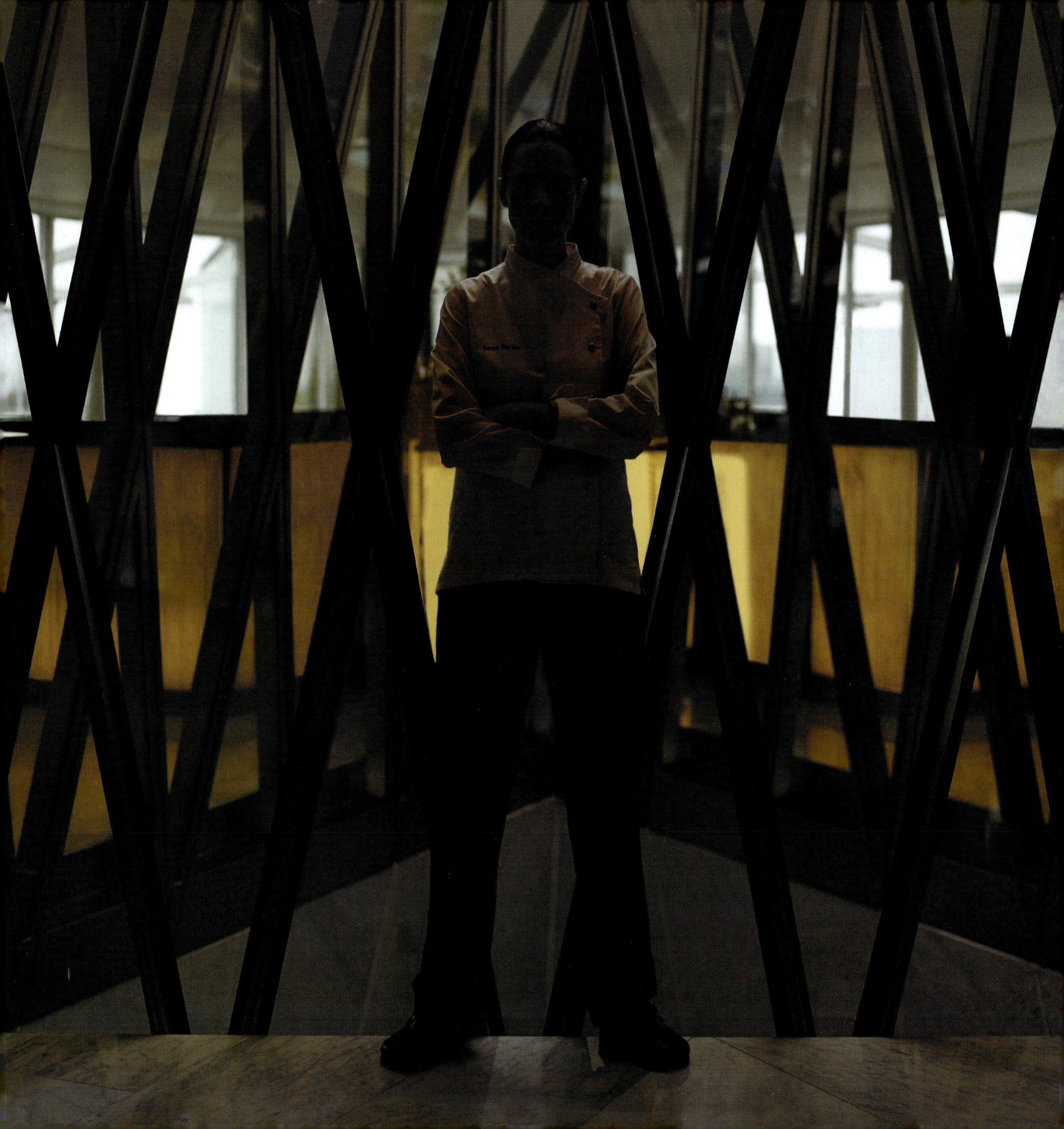

SB

SARAH BARBER
Patisserie Perfection

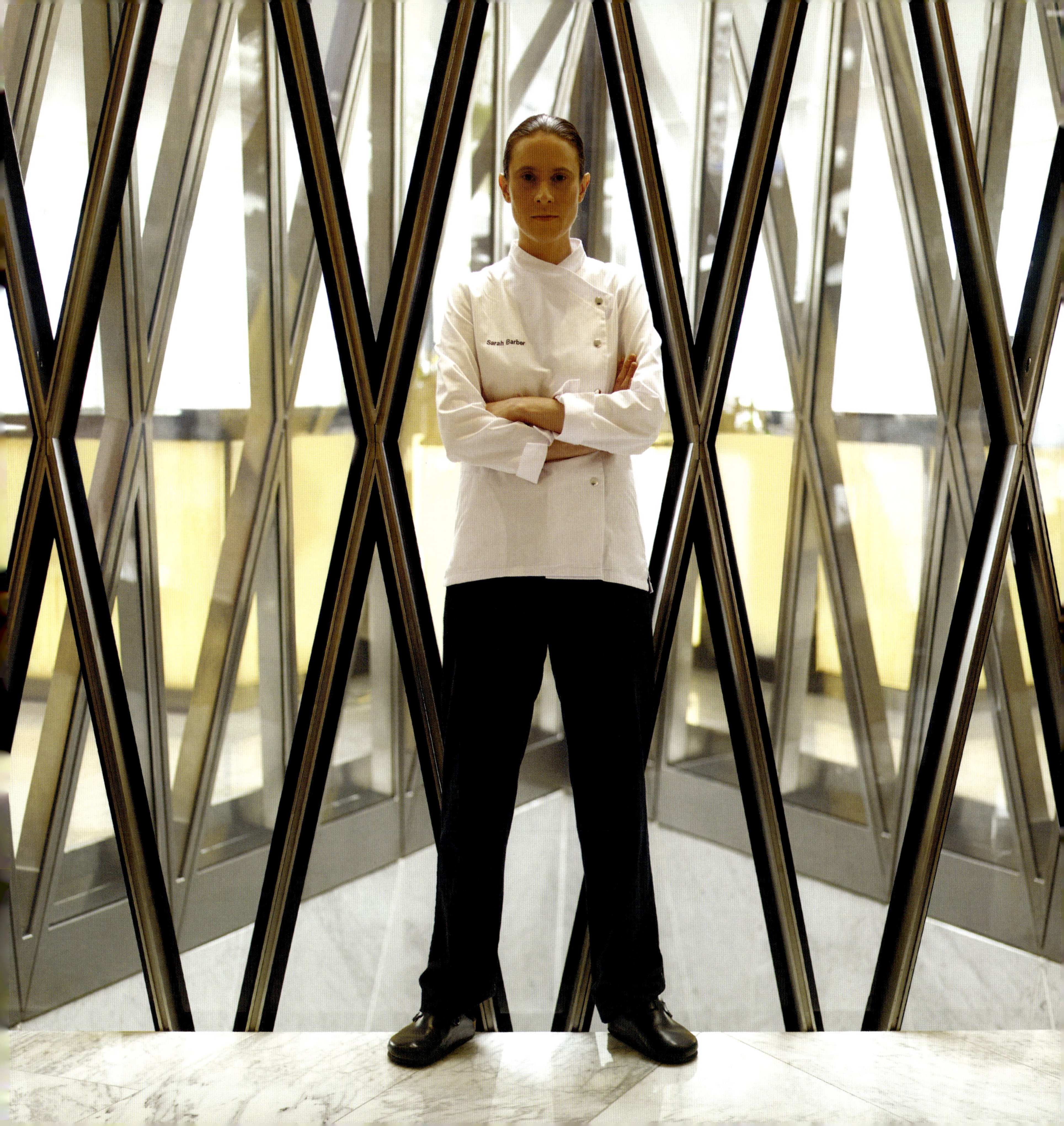
Sarah Barber

London, June 2009 - a young pastry chef walks into my brigade. Little did I know back then what would come from them and how they would grow. I required a general, a quality enforcer and an additional level of organisation. Sarah Barber was the chef in question and she came with a presence! The pastry kitchen at Mandarin Oriental, Hyde Park was a tough and demanding culinary arena. You had to learn quickly and standards were high and unrelenting. With plenty of opportunity to grow, Sarah swiftly adapted and attained a reputation for no nonsense cooking. Whilst proving her collective abilities of solid administration, good practical skills and huge passion she demonstrated her hunger for knowledge. As such she was installed in December 2010 as the pastry chef to open Dinner by Heston Blumenthal where she remained until August 2011.Yauatcha, Hakkasan Group, August 2011 - the rebirth of this U.K leader in patisserie was very much down to Sarah and her teams. A massively difficult kitchen and even more demanding group chef, perfection was required and delivered under immense duress. Blood, sugar and tears helped to forge a new and enhanced reputation, achieved through the patisserie retail of this Michelin-starred Soho restaurant. Global growth and increased productivity saw the commissioning of a production kitchen of which Sarah also opened.

In my twenty-five years as a chef I have worked with and helped develop some of the best young pastry chefs who operate around the globe. I consider myself very fortunate to mentor and guide these individuals and to their collective benefit seen them achieve huge success. Sarah is another of these chefs and is driven, passionate and professional. She has a wealth of knowledge and demonstrates this through these pages. Obsessive with the future of our profession and the development of the next generation of chefs, she now shares some of this knowledge with you.

Graham Hornigold
Executive Pastry Chef, Hakkasan group

During my professional career as a pastry chef and chocolatier, I've been privileged to work with and train many great chefs from around the world. My time competing in international culinary competition, most recently representing the UK at the World Chocolate Masters, has provided me with an rare insight into the emerging talent within the industry. Sarah Barber is one such talent. I first met Sarah three years ago when I was training for the World Chocolate Masters. It was a very busy time in my life. We had just launched Cocoa Black and I was still finding my feet as a new mother. Despite all of this, it was immediately apparent that Sarah had the passion and talent needed to succeed as a pastry chef. I met her again last year when she visited us at the Chocolate & Pastry School in Peebles and was delighted to see how her work had evolved and matured into her own recognisable style. When Sarah asked me to write a foreword for her book, I was happy to oblige. Not least because I respect her as a chef, but also because I feel that her recipes should be made widely available for others to enjoy. In writing this book, Sarah has set out to challenge and inspire young professionals. To this end, I hope that she will achieve her goal, and it's satisfying to know that her recipes will be enjoyed far and wide.

Ruth Hinks
UK World Chocolate Master

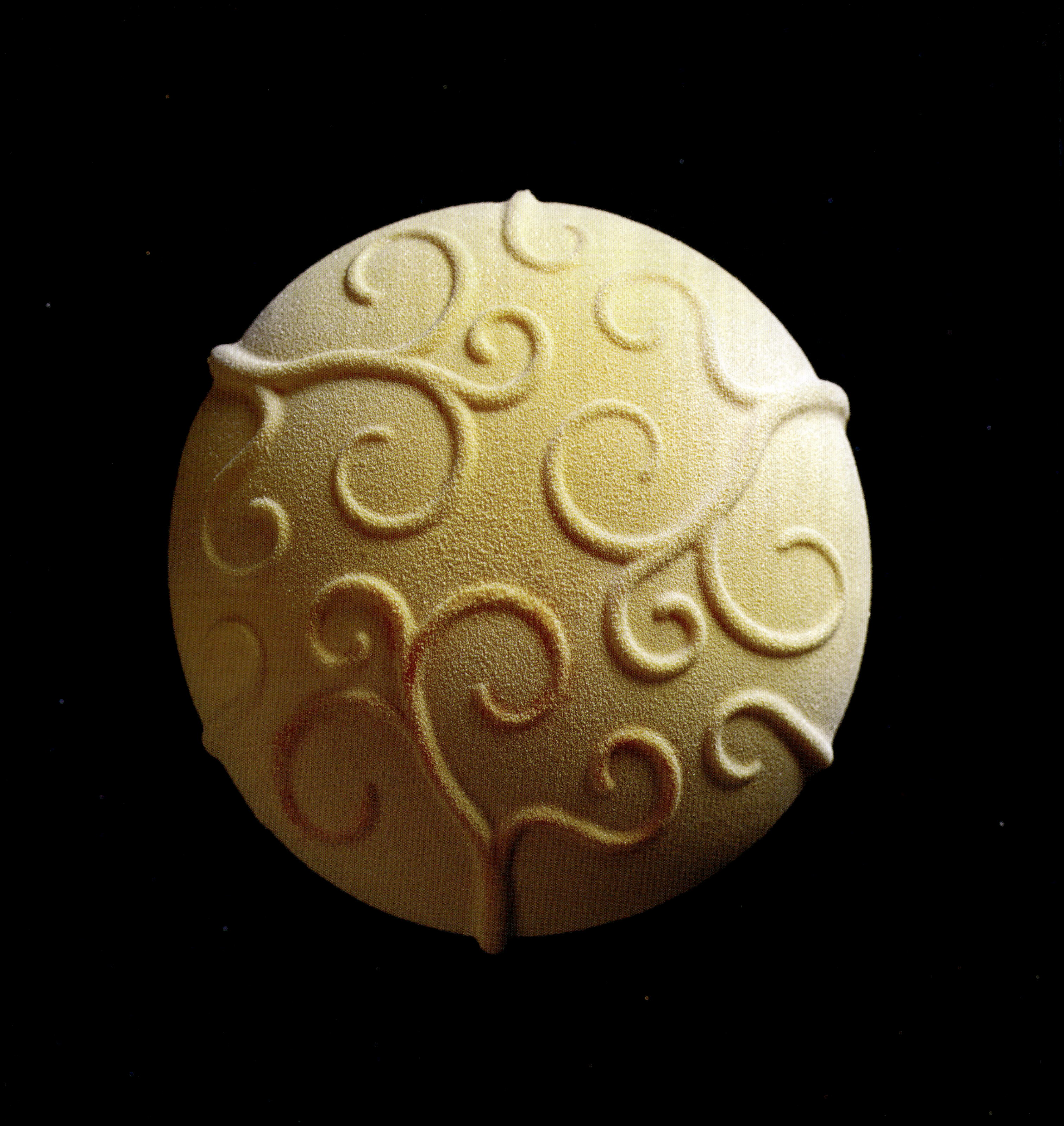

Contents:

Chocolates 10

Deconstructed Desserts 50

Entremets 66

Small Sweets 92

Petit Gateaux 114

Chocolate Bars 134

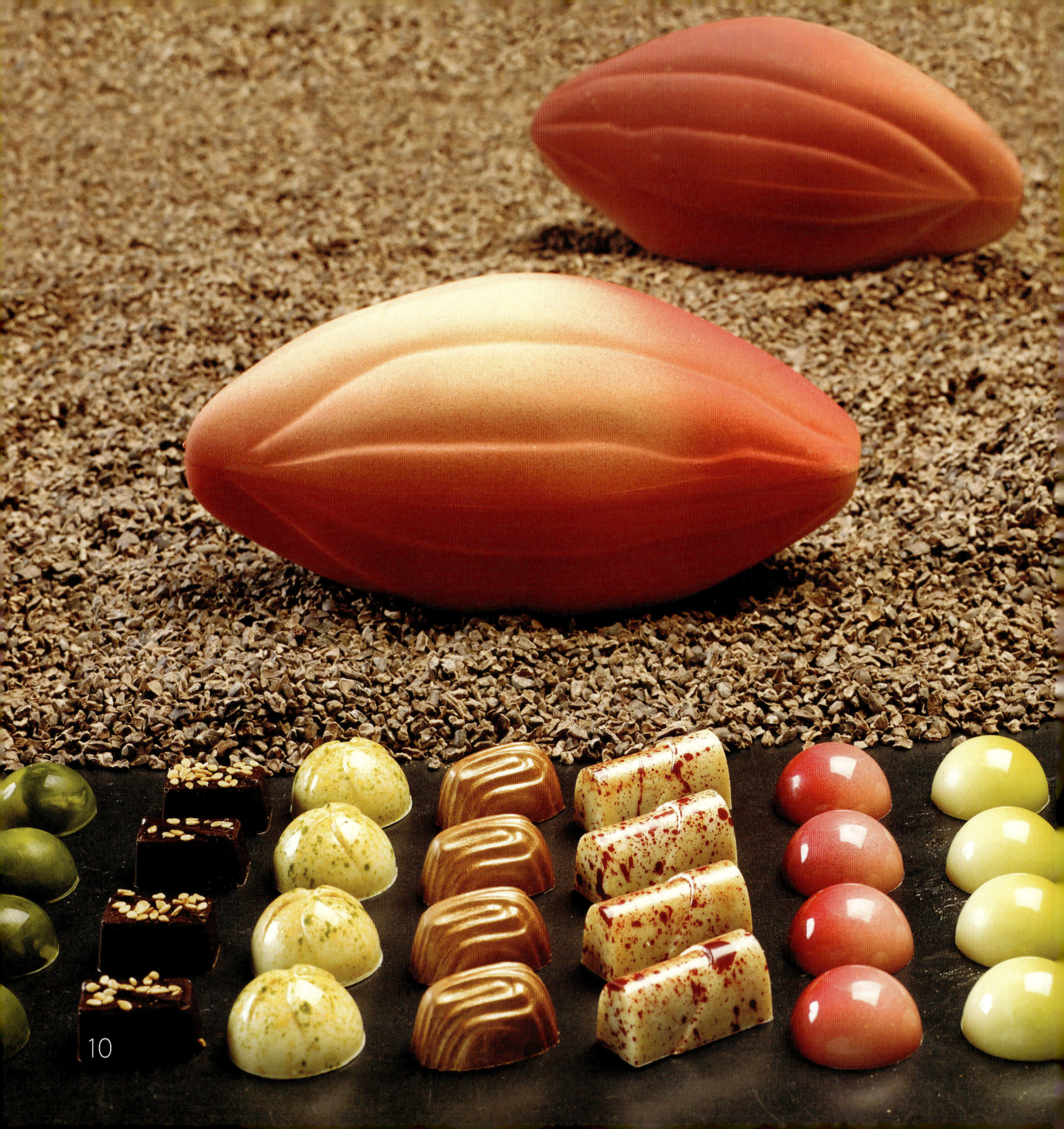

Chocolates

Wild Strawberry

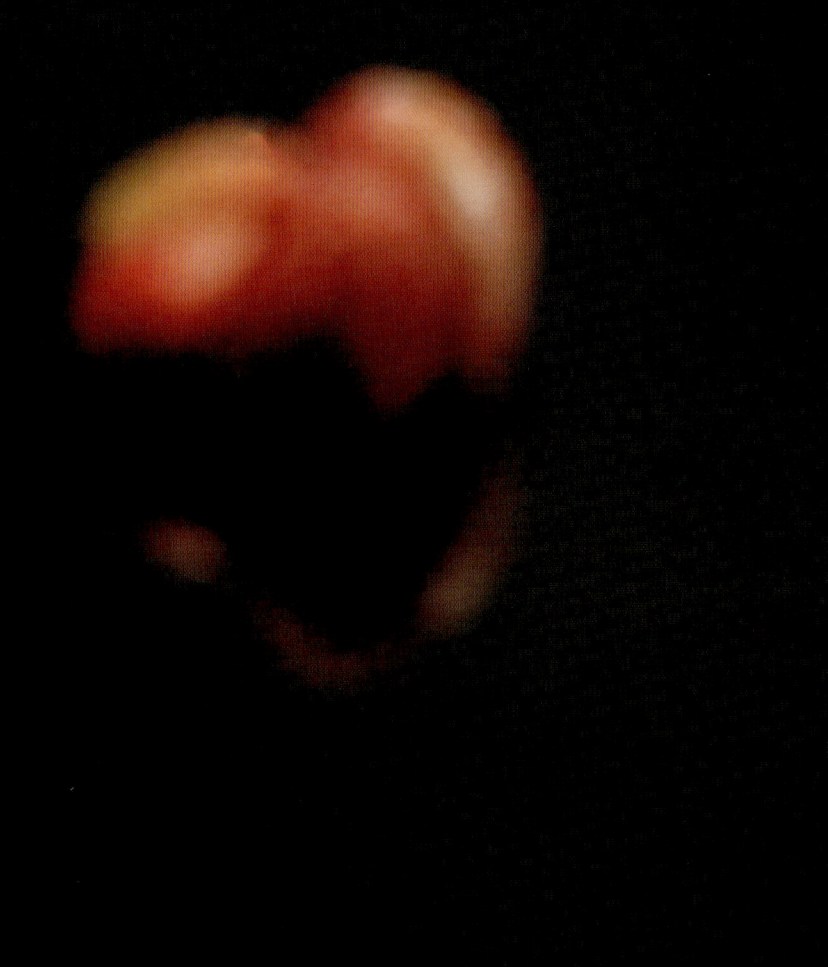

WILD STRAWBERRY GANACHE

300g wild strawberry purée, 285g Opayls 33% white chocolate, 50g unsalted butter, 1.5g citric acid, 0.5g strawberry sevarome colour, 10g liquid sorbitol inverted sugar

Mix the strawberry purée with the colour and reduce to 170g. Melt the chocolate to 45°C. Add the liquid sorbitol inverted sugar to the chocolate, then add the boiling purée in three stages. Place in a Thermomix on a slow speed and gradually add the butter. Add the citric acid at the end. Mix until emulsified and a smooth ganache is formed. Place into a piping bag and pipe into moulds at 28°C.

FOR CASTING THE MOULD

Brush the polished moulds with pink cocoa butter at 29°C until a even layer is formed. Temper the Opalys white chocolate and pour into the mould to cast. The following day pipe the ganache into the moulds and leave overnight to crystallise. The next day temper the white chocolate and use to seal the base of the chocolates. Once ready, de mould them.

Lavender & Honey

LAVENDER HONEY GANACHE

260g whipping cream, 3g picked fresh lavender, 70g wild honey, 250g Ashanti, 67% dark chocolate, 90g unsalted butter, 20g liquid sorbitol inverted sugar

Bring the cream to the boil, take off the heat add the picked lavender seeds. Clingfilm the pan and leave to infuse for 20 minutes. Place the honey in separate pan and caramelise. Once smoking, deglaze the pan with the lavender cream and bring back to the boil. Melt the chocolate to 45°, add the liquid sorbitol inverted sugar to the chocolate. Pass the honey lavender cream through a fine chinois and pour over the chocolate in three stages. Place in a Thermomix on a slow speed and gradually add the butter. Mix until emulsified and a smooth ganache is formed. Place into a piping bag and pipe into moulds at 29°C.

FOR CASTING THE MOULD

Flick the polished moulds with a brush using purple cocoa butter at 29°C. Temper the Opalys white chocolate and pour into the mould to cast. The following day pipe the ganache into the moulds and leave overnight to crystallise. The next day temper the white chocolate and use to seal the base of the chocolates. Once ready de mould them.

Chocolates 15

16 Chocolates

Mandarin Orange Blossom

MANDARIN BLOSSOM GANACHE

300g Mandarin purée, 100g whipping cream, 8g Orange Blossom Essence, 5g Orange zest, 250g Caraibe 66% dark chocolate, 90g Unsalted Butter, 15g Liquid Sorbitol inverted sugar

Mix the Mandarin purée with the zest and reduce to 175g. Once reduced bring to the boil with the cream and essence. Melt the chocolate to 45°C, add the inverted sugar. Gradually add the liquid in three stages to the chocolates, emulsifying each time. Place in a Thermomix on a slow speed and gradually add the butter. Mix until emulsified and a smooth ganache is formed. Place into a piping bag and pipe into moulds at 29°C.

FOR CASTING THE MOULD

Brush the polished moulds evenly using orange cocoa butter at 29°C. Temper the Caraibe dark chocolate and pour into the mould to cast. The following day pipe the ganache into the moulds and leave overnight to crystallise. The next day temper the dark chocolate and use to seal the base of the chocolates. Once ready de mould them.

Blackcurrant Violet

BLACKCURRANT VIOLET GANACHE

160g blackcurrant purée, 20g whole milk, 285g Opayls 33% White chocolate, 50g unsalted butter, 2g citric acid, 3g blitzed violets, 10g violet crispies, 10g liquid sorbitol inverted sugar

Bring the purée, milk and blitzed violets to the boil. Melt the chocolate to 45°C, add the inverted sugar pour the purée mix in three stages over the chocolate. With a hand blender add the butter and citric acid and emulsify to a smooth ganache. Once at 28°C fold in the violet crispies with a spatula and place in piping bags. Pipe into moulds.

FOR CASTING THE MOULD

Flick the polished moulds, using a brush, with a light purple cocoa butter at 29°C. Temper the Opalys white chocolate and pour into the mould to cast. The following day pipe the ganache into the moulds and leave overnight to crystallise. The next day temper the white chocolate and use to seal the base of the chocolates. Once ready de mould them.

Chocolates 19

20 Chocolates

Fresh Mint

FRESH MINT GANACHE

270g whipping cream, 5g fresh picked mint, 250g Guanaja, 70% dark chocolate, 90g unsalted butter, 25g Trimoline inverted sugar

Place the cream and fresh mint in the Thermomix, place on Varoma and warm to 90°C for 15 minutes. Melt the chocolate to 45°C, add the inverted sugar to the chocolate. Pass the cream mix through a fine chinois and pour over the chocolate in three stages. Emulsify the ganache with the butter with a hand blender until smooth and glossy. Pipe into moulds at 29°C.

FOR CASTING THE MOULD

Brush the polished with a dark green cocoa butter at 29°C. Temper the Guanaja dark chocolate and pour into the mould to cast. The following day pipe the ganache into the moulds and leave overnight to crystallise. The next day temper the dark chocolate and use to seal the base of the chocolates. Once ready de mould them.

Lemon Thyme

LEMON THYME GANACHE

270g whipping cream, 10g picked lemon thyme, 250g Caraibe 66% dark chocolate, 90g butter, 15g liquid sorbitol inverted sugar

Bring the cream to the boil, remove from the heat and add the lemon thyme. Clingfilm the pan and leave to infuse for 20 minutes. Melt the chocolate to 45°C, add the inverted sugar. Bring the cream back to the boil, pass through a fine chinois. Pour over the chocolate and add the liquid in three stages. Emulsify the ganache with the butter with a hand blender until smooth and glossy. Pipe into moulds at 29°C.

FOR CASTING THE MOULD

Brush the polished with a light green cocoa butter at 29°C. Temper the Opalys white chocolate and pour into the mould to cast. The following day pipe the ganache into the moulds and leave overnight to crystallise. The next day temper the white chocolate and use to seal the base of the chocolates. Once ready de mould them.

Chocolates 23

Burnt Sugar

BURNT SUGAR GANACHE

160g whipping cream, 285g Dulcey 32% milk chocolate, 100g palm sugar, 10g demerara sugar, 50g unsalted butter, 10g liquid sorbitol inverted sugar

Place the cream in a pan and bring to the boil. In a separate pan place the palm sugar and melt until dissolved. At this stage, add the demerara sugar and turn to a high heat until golden brown and caramelised. Deglaze the caramel with the hot cream gradually, until a thick, dark brown caramel cream is formed. Melt the chocolate to 45°C, add the inverted sugar. Add the caramel cream to the chocolate gradually. Place in a Thermomix on a slow speed and gradually add the butter. Mix until emulsified and a smooth ganache is formed. Place into a piping bag and pipe into moulds at 28°C.

FOR CASTING THE MOULD

Brush the mould with gold shimmer. Temper the Caraibe dark chocolate and pour into the mould to cast. The following day pipe the ganache into the moulds and leave overnight to crystallise. The next day temper the dark chocolate and use to seal the base of the chocolates. Once ready de mould them.

Chocolates 25

Salted Peanut

PEANUT PASTE

200g roasted salted peanuts, 25g peanut oil

Roast the peanuts in an oven at 180°C until dark golden brown, Place in a Thermomix and blend on a high speed, gradually adding the oil until a smooth paste is formed.

SALTED PEANUT GANACHE

150g peanut paste, 120g whipping cream, 250g Tanariva 33% milk chocolate, 90g unsalted Butter, 15g liquid sorbitol inverted sugar

Bring the peanut paste and the cream to the boil. Melt the chocolate to 45°C, add the inverted sugar. Add the cream paste gradually and stir well. Emulsify the ganache with the butter, with a hand blender, until smooth and glossy. Pipe into moulds at 28°C.

FOR CASTING THE MOULD

Brush the mould with a bronze cocoa butter colour at 29°C. Temper the Caraibe dark chocolate and pour into the mould to cast. The following day pipe the ganache into the moulds and leave overnight to crystallise. The next day temper the dark chocolate and use to seal the base of the chocolates. Once ready de mould them.

Chocolates 27

28 Chocolates

Spiced Anise

SPICED ANISE GANACHE

270g whipping cream, 3g star anise, 3g cinnamon sticks, 2g cardamon seeds, 2g juniper berries, 250g Caramelia 36% milk chocolate, 90g unsalted butter, 15g trimoline inverted sugar

Roast the cinnamon, cardamon, juniper berries and star anise in a dry pan on a high heat, until the aroma is released. Add the cream and bring back to the boil. Place in an airtight container and leave refrigerated for 12 hours. Melt the chocolate to 45°C, add the inverted sugar. Bring the liquid with the spices back to the boil, pass through a fine chinois and pour over the chocolate in three stages. Place in a Thermomix on a slow speed and gradually add the butter. Mix until emulsified and a smooth ganache is formed. Place into a piping bag and pipe into moulds at 28°C.

FOR CASTING THE MOULD

Brush the mould with red and bronze shimmer powders. Temper the Caraibe dark chocolate and pour into the mould to cast. The following day pipe the ganache into the moulds and leave overnight to crystallise. The next day temper the dark chocolate and use to seal the base of the chocolates. Once ready de mould them.

Lemon Basil

LEMON BASIL GANACHE

170g whipping cream, 6g fresh picked basil, 2g lemon zest, 285g Opalys 33% white chocolate, 50g unsalted butter, 10g liquid sorbitol Inverted sugar

Place the cream, basil and lemon zest in the Thermomix, place on Varoma and warm to 90°C for 15 minutes. Pass through a fine chinois. Melt the chocolate to 45°C, add the inverted sugar. Gradually pour in the basil cream, adding in three stages. Emulsify the ganache with the butter, with a hand blender, until smooth and glossy. Pipe into moulds at 28°C.

FOR CASTING THE MOULD

Flick the mould, using a brush, with citrus yellow and light green coloured cocoa butters. Temper the Opalys white chocolate and pour into the mould to cast. The following day pipe the ganache into the moulds and leave overnight to crystallise. The next day temper the white chocolate and use to seal the base of the chocolates. Once ready de mould them.

Chocolates 31

Sesame

SESAME SEED PASTE

150g roasted sesame seeds, 40g sesame oil

Roast the sesame seeds, until golden brown in an oven at 180°C. Place in a Thermomix with the oil and blend to a smooth paste.

SESAME SEED GANACHE

130g sesame seed paste, 140g whipping cream, 250g Abinao 58% dark chocolate, 90g unsalted butter, 20g liquid sorbitol inverted sugar

Bring the sesame paste and cream to the boil, melt the chocolate to 45°C, add the inverted sugar. Add the cream paste in three stages. Place in a Thermomix on a slow speed and gradually add the butter. Mix until emulsified and a smooth ganache is formed. Place into a piping bag and pipe into moulds at 28°C.

FOR CASTING THE MOULD

Temper the Caraibe dark chocolate and pour into the mould to cast. The following day pipe the ganache into the moulds and leave overnight to crystallise. The next day temper the dark chocolate and use to seal the base of the chocolates. Once ready de mould them. Decorate with toasted sesame seeds.

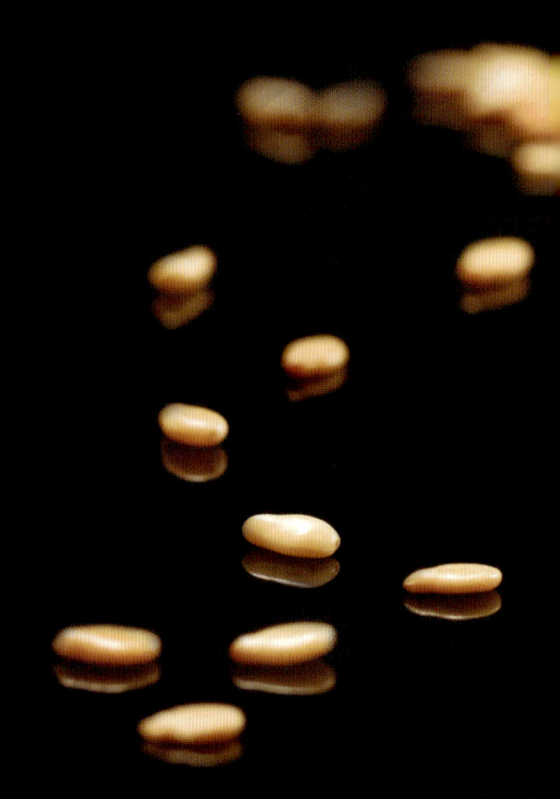

Chocolates 33

Tonka Bean

TONKA BEAN GANACHE

260g whipping cream, 3g blitzed Tonka beans, 250g Biskella 34% milk chocolate, 90g unsalted butter, 20g Trimoline inverted sugar, 10g chocolate croquant

Bring the cream to the boil, remove from the heat and add the blitzed Tonka beans. Clingfilm the pan and leave to infuse for 20 minutes. Melt the chocolate to 45°C add the inverted sugar. Bring the Tonka cream back to the boil and pass through muslin cloth. Add the cream to the chocolate in three stages. Place in a Thermomix on a slow speed and gradually add the butter. Mix until emulsified and a smooth ganache is formed. Fold through the chocolate croquant. Place into a piping bag and pipe into moulds at 28°C.

FOR CASTING THE MOULD

Temper the Caraibe dark chocolate and pour into the mould to cast. The following day pipe the ganache into the moulds and leave overnight to crystallise. The next day temper the dark chocolate and use to seal the base of the chocolates. Once ready de mould them. Lightly spray with gold shimmer.

Chocolates 35

Coconut Lemongrass

COCONUT LEMONGRASS GANACHE

220g coconut milk, 20g blitzed fresh lemongrass, 8g toasted desiccated coconut, 10g Malibu rum, 285g Opayls 33% white chocolate, 50g unsalted butter, 10g liquid sorbitol inverted sugar

Chop the lemongrass Place in a Thermomix and blitz to a paste. Add to the cold coconut cream and Malibu and keep in airtight container refrigerated for 12 hours. Bring back to the boil, pass through a muslin cloth. Melt the chocolate to 45°C add the inverted sugar, pour the coconut cream mix over the chocolate in three stages. Emulsify the ganache with the butter with a hand blender until smooth and glossy. Fold through the toasted Desiccated coconut and mix well. Pipe into moulds at 28°C.

FOR CASTING THE MOULD

Place the transfer sheet in the magnetic mould and press evenly. Temper the Caraibe dark chocolate and pour into the mould to cast. The following day pipe the ganache into the moulds and leave overnight to crystallise. The next day temper the dark chocolate and use to seal the base of the chocolates. Once ready de mould them.

Chocolates 37

Passionfruit, Ginger Salt

GINGER GANACHE

270g whipping cream, 12g fresh grated ginger, 250g Araguani, 72% dark chocolate, 90g unsalted butter, 3g ginger salt, 15g Trimoline inverted sugar

Grate the fresh ginger into the cold cream and stir well. Place in an airtight container and leave refrigerated for 12 hours. The next day bring back to the boil and pass through a fine chinois. Melt the chocolate to 45°C then add the inverted sugar. Gradually add the ginger cream in three stages. Place in a Thermomix on a slow speed and gradually add the butter. Mix until emulsified and a smooth ganache is formed, add the salt last. Place into a piping bag and pipe into moulds at 30°C.

GINGER SALT

25g Maldon sea salt, 10g fresh grated ginger

Blitz the ginger and salt together until they are mixed well. Sprinkle onto a silpat mat and dry in a dehydrator overnight or in an oven at 60°C for 6 hours. Once dry crush and store in an airtight container.

PASSIONFRUIT PATE D' FRUIT

160g passionfruit purée, 100g caster sugar, 20g fresh orange juice, 5g yellow pectin, 30g liquid glucose, 1.5g citric acid, 1g water

Bring the passionfruit purée and orange juice to the boil, add the glucose. Mix the yellow pectin and caster sugar together, gradually pour into the boiling liquid, whisking constantly. Cook this to 105°C. Mix the citric acid and the water and add this to the liquid. Pour into a tray lined with a silicone mat. Once set, cut into small discs to place in between the crystallised ganache.

FOR CASTING THE MOULD

Flick the mould, using a brush, with yellow cocoa butter at 29°C. Temper the Caraibe dark chocolate and pour into the mould to cast. The following day pipe the ganache into the moulds, filling half way, then pipe the passionfruit pate d' fruit, followed by more ganache. Leave overnight to crystallise. The next day temper the dark chocolate and use to seal the base of the chocolates. Once ready de mould them.

Raspberry Rose

40 Chocolates

RASPBERRY ROSE GANACHE

250g raspberry purée, 285g Opayls 33% white chocolate, 1g rose essence, 2g citric acid, 2g raspberry Sevarome colour, 50g unsalted butter, 10g liquid sorbitol inverted sugar, 10g rose crispies

Reduce the purée to 170g, melt the chocolate to 45°C then add the inverted sugar. Add the purée in three stages. Once mixed place in the Thermomix. Gradually add the butter on a low speed. Once emulsified, add the raspberry colour and the citric acid. Place the ganache into a bowl. When at 29°C, fold through the rose crispies. Pipe into moulds at 28°C.

FOR CASTING THE MOULD

Airbrush the mould using red and light pink coloured cocoa butters, at 29°C. Temper the Opalys white chocolate and pour into the mould to cast. The following day pipe the ganache into the moulds leave overnight to crystallise. The next day temper the white chocolate and use to seal the bottom of the mould. Once ready de mould.

Tahiti Vanilla

TAHITI VANILLA GANACHE

160g whipping cream, 3 Tahiti vanilla pods, cut and deseeded, 285g Opayls, 33% white chocolate, 2g acidic yoghurt powder, 50g unsalted butter, 10g liquid sorbitol inverted sugar

Bring the cream, vanilla seeds and pods to the boil, and whisk well. Melt the chocolate to 45°C, add the inverted sugar. Pass the vanilla cream through a muslin cloth, over the chocolate, adding in three stages. Emulsify the ganache with the butter and the yoghurt powder, with a hand blender, until smooth. Pipe into moulds at 28°C.

FOR CASTING THE MOULD

Brush the moulds with a light sliver shimmer powder. Temper the Opalys white chocolate and pour into the mould to cast. The following day, pipe the ganache into the moulds leave overnight to crystallise. Temper the white chocolate and use to seal the bottom of the mould. Once ready de mould.

Chocolates 43

44 Chocolates

Matcha

MATCHA GANACHE

170g whipping cream, 8g Matcha powder, 4g lemon zest, 2g fresh lemon juice, 285g Opayls 33% white chocolate, 50g unsalted butter, 10g liquid sorbitol inverted sugar

Bring the cream and lemon zest to the boil, remove from heat and whisk in the matcha powder. Clingfilm the pan and leave to infuse for 15 minutes. Bring back to the boil and pass through a muslin cloth. Melt the chocolate to 45°C, add the inverted sugar. Pour the matcha lemon cream over the chocolate in three stages. Emulsify the ganache with the butter, with a hand blender, until smooth. Add the lemon juice and blitz again with the hand blender. Pipe into moulds at 28°C.

FOR CASTING THE MOULD

Airbrush the moulds with a green cocoa butter at 29°C. Temper the Opalys white chocolate and pour into the mould to cast. The following day pipe the ganache into the moulds. Leave overnight to crystallise. Temper the white chocolate and use to seal the bottom of the mould. Once ready de mould.

Hibiscus

HIBISCUS GANACHE

180g whipping cream, 12g dried hibiscus, 285g Manjari, 64% dark chocolate, 50g unsalted butter, 10g liquid sorbitol inverted sugar

Bring the cream to the boil, remove from the heat and add the hibiscus. Clingfilm and leave to infuse for 30 minutes. Bring back to the boil and pass through a fine chinois. Melt the chocolate to 45°C then add the inverted sugar. Add the cream to the chocolate in 3 stages, mixing each time until glossy and smooth. Place in a Thermomix and, on a low speed, add the softened butter. Blend until the ganache is emulsified. Pipe into moulds at 28°C.

FOR CASTING THE MOULD

Flick the moulds, using a brush, with red and yellow coloured cocoa butters, at 29°C. Temper the Opalys white chocolate and pour into the mould to cast. The following day pipe the ganache into the moulds leave overnight to crystallise. Temper the white chocolate and use to seal the bottom of the mould. Once ready de mould.

Mango Caramel Lime

MANGO CARAMEL LIME GANACHE

200g mango purée, 60g whipping cream, 100g caster sugar, 3g Malden sea salt, 2g lime zest, 4g lime juice, 250g Jivaria milk chocolate, 90g butter, 15g liquid sorbitol inverted sugar

Make a direct caramel with the sugar. Once a clear golden brown colour, deglaze with the whipping cream, mango purée, salt and lime zest. Bring back to the boil. Melt the chocolate to 45°C, add the inverted sugar then add the mango caramel cream in three stages. Place in a Thermomix, adding the butter gradually, on a low speed, to emulsify. Add the lime juice at the end. Pipe into moulds at 28°C.

FOR CASTING THE MOULD

Brush the moulds using yellow and gold coloured cocoa butters, at 29°C. Temper the Opalys white chocolate and pour into the mould to cast. The following day pipe the ganache into the moulds leave overnight to crystallise. Temper the white chocolate and use to seal the bottom of the mould. Once ready de mould.

Chocolates 49

Deconstructed Desserts

51

Black Forest Gateau

Deconstructed Desserts 53

CHERRY GEL

100g sour cherry purée, 10g Kirsch, 1g agar agar, 20g icing sugar

Bring the cherry purée and the kirsch to the boil, mix the agar agar and the icing sugar together, gradually pour into the boiling liquid and whisk well. Bring back to the boil, once boiling pour onto a silicone mat to set. Once set place into a Thermomix and blend to a smooth paste. Bag ready for use.

CHOCOLATE SPONGE

168g egg whites, 72g caster sugar, 96g egg yolks, 74g T55 soft flour, 30g cocoa powder, 2g salt, 48g softened butter

Make a french meringue with the egg whites and sugar in a mixing machine, adding the sugar in two stages until a stiff peak meringue is formed. Sieve the cocoa powder and flour together and salt. Add the egg yolks to the meringue, add the softened butter and whisk till smooth. Finally, with the machine on a low speed, gradually add the cocoa powder and flour, whisking until smooth. Spread onto a silicone mat and bake at 175°C for 9 minutes. Cut into cubes and roll in cocoa powder.

CHOCOLATE CHERRY MOUSSE

114g Zephr 34% white chocolate, 40g caster sugar, 20g whole eggs, 20g egg yolks, 10g water, 4g gelatine, 90g sour cherry purée, 110g whipping cream

Melt the chocolate to 40°C. Make a pâte à bombe with the whole eggs, yolks, sugar and water. Boil the cherry purée, add the bloomed gelatine and stir well. Whip the cream to ribbon stage. Fold the purée into the pâte à bombe, then fold through the chocolate and finally the whipped cream. Pipe into quenelle moulds to freeze.

CHOCOLATE SOIL

600g caster sugar, 120g water, 280g Alto El sol 65% dark chocolate

Melt the chocolate to 40°C. Cook the sugar and water to 121°C. Pour in the melted chocolate and whisk rapidly on the heat until the sugar crystallises and small chocolate rocks are formed. Pour onto a silicone mat to cool.

KIRSCH PANNACOTTA

112g whipping cream, 27g whole milk, 10g Kirsch, 2 Tahiti vanilla pods, 3g gelatine

Bring the milk, cream, Kirsch and vanilla pod seeds to the boil. Add the bloomed gelatine stir well. Pass through a muslin cloth and leave the mixture to set on an ice bath so the vanilla is immersed. Once set, pour into quenelle moulds to set.

POACHED CHERRIES

100g sour cherry purée, 300g simple syrup, 1 Tahiti vanilla pod, 50g Kirsch, 200g fresh cherries

Cut the cherries in half. Bring the purée, syrup, kirsch and vanilla to the boil. Pour over the fresh cherry halves and leave to marinade.

WHIPPED CHOCOLATE GANACHE

250g whipping cream, 25g glucose, 30g caster sugar, 160g Alto El Sol 65% chocolate, 375g whipping cream

Make a direct caramel with the sugar. Once a clear golden brown, add the glucose and stir well. Deglaze with the 250g of whipping cream and bring back to the boil. Melt the chocolate to 40°C and pour the caramel cream gradually, in 3 stages, to the chocolate. Once smooth and glossy, add the remaining 375g whipping cream and stir well with a spatula. Pour into an airtight container and leave refrigerated for 12 hours. The next day place in a mixing machine and whisk to form a soft, whipped chocolate ganache. Pipe into lollipop moulds and freeze.

LOLLIPOP DIPPING MIX

250g Alto de sol 65% dark chocolate, 200g cocoa butter

Melt both chocolates to 40°C, mix together and pass through a fine chinos. De-mould the ganache lollipops and immerse in the mix.

Deconstructed Desserts

Peach Melba

PEACH MOUSSE

250g peach purée reduced to 150g, 20g egg yolks, 4.5g gelatine, 20g egg whites, 30g caster sugar, 150g whipping cream

Reduce the purée, whisk the egg yolks, pour the purée onto the egg yolks and whisk. Return to the pan and cook to 75°C then add the bloomed gelatine and whisk well. Chill this base to 25°C. Make an Italian meringue and fold into the base. Whisk the cream to ribbon stage, and fold this through last. Pipe into moulds.

VANILLA PARFAIT

40g caster sugar, 15g water, 35g egg yolks, 3g gelatine, 3 Tahiti vanilla pods, 180g whipping cream

Make a pâte à bombe, once the sugar syrup reaches 121°C add the bloomed gelatine. Pour this syrup over the egg yolks, add the vanilla seeds at this stage. Whisk to a stiff sabayon. Separately whisk the cream to ribbon stage, fold into the pate bombe, mixing well. Pipe into moulds to freeze.

PEACH SAUCE

100g peach purée, 1g ultratex

Place the peach purée and ultratex in a small jug and blend with a hand blender until the purée thickens. Bag ready to use.

ALMOND FINANCIER

295g butter, 300g egg whites, 1g salt, 50g inverted sugar, 310g icing sugar, 100g T55 soft flour, 100g ground almonds

Place the butter in pan and take to brown butter stage, leave aside. Whisk the egg whites and icing sugar, gradually adding the sugar in three stages, whisk to a stiff meringue. Sieve the almonds, salt and flour. Add the inverted sugar to the meringue and then pour in the dry ingredients, in two stages. Finally add the warm brown butter. Place the mix in an airtight container and refrigerate for 2 hours before baking. Pipe into moulds and bake at 175°C for 8 minutes.

RASPBERRY CRISPA

100g raspberry purée, 25g icing sugar, 2g gelatine

Boil the purée and the icing sugar, add the bloomed gelatine and stir well. Spread onto a slicone mat and dry in a dehydrator overnight or in an oven at 70°C for 4 hours. Once dry break into pieces and store in an airtight container.

ALMOND PUREE

50g whole roasted almonds, 280g whole milk

Roast the almonds in an oven at 175°C for 12 minutes until dark golden brown. Bring the milk to the boil. Place the almonds and the milk in a Thermomix and blend on a high speed until a smooth paste is formed. Bag ready to use.

ALMOND SOIL

50g maltosec, 25g almond oil

Whisk together to form a almond powder. Bag ready to use.

Deconstructed Desserts

Eton Mess

STRAWBERRY MERINGUES

100g egg whites, 190g caster sugar, 5g cornflour, 20g blitzed strawberry crispies

Whisk the egg whites on a mixing machine gradually adding the sugar in 3 stages until a stiff meringue is formed, then add the cornflour and whisk again. On a silicone mat pipe thin lines and sprinkle with the crispies. Place in a dehydrator overnight on 60°C.

VANILLA MOUSSE

125g whole milk, 125g whipping cream, 40g egg yolks, 5g caster sugar, 2 Bourbon vanilla pods, 6g gelatine, 250g whipping cream, 15g egg whites, 25g caster sugar, 8g water

Whip the 250g whipping cream to ribbon stage. Make an Anglaise with the milk, cream, yolks, sugar and vanilla seeds and pods. Cook to 75°C. Add the bloomed gelatine and stir well, pass through a fine chinois and cool this base to 25°C. Make an Italian meringue with the whites, sugar and water. Once cool, fold the meringue into the base and finally add the whipped cream. Pipe into moulds to set.

STRAWBERRY MOUSSE

250g strawberry purée, 40g egg yolks, 5g caster sugar, 6g gelatine, 250g whipping cream, 15g egg whites, 25g caster sugar, 8g water

Whip the 250g whipping cream to ribbon stage. Make an Anglaise with the purée, yolks and sugar and cook to 75°C. Add the bloomed gelatine and stir well, pass through a fine chinois and cool this base to 25°C. Make an Italian meringue with the whites, sugar and water. Once cool, fold the meringue into the base and finally add the whipped cream. Pipe into moulds to set.

STRAWBERRY SPRAY

250g Zephyr white chocolate, 110g cocoa butter, 10g red cocoa butter, 10g white cocoa butter

Melt the chocolate and cocoa butters separately to 40°C. Mix together and then pass through a muslin cloth. Place into a spray gun and use at 35°C.

POACHED STRAWBERRIES

100g simple syrup, 2g lemon zest, 1 Tahiti vanilla pod de-seeded, 100g wild strawberries

Bring the simple syrup, lemon zest and vanilla to the boil. Pour over the strawberries and leave for 1 hour to marinade.

STRAWBERRY SAUCE

100g strawberry purée, 1g ultratex, 1g lemon juice

Blend all ingredients together with a hand blender until smooth. Bag ready for use.

Deconstructed Desserts 59

Lemon Meringue Pie

SMASHED TART SWEET PASTRY

135g T55 soft flour, 70g unsalted butter, 45g caster sugar, 40g whole eggs, 20g egg yolks,1g salt

Cream the butter and sugar together, then add the whole eggs, yolks and salt and work to a smooth paste. Add the flour and mix until the dough comes together. Clingfilm and rest for one hour. Line a small tart ring and blind bake for 10 mins at 165°C. Remove the beans and bake for a further 5 minutes at 170°C.

LEMON CURD

150g lemon juice, 12g lemon zest, 170g unsalted butter, 180g whole eggs, 60g egg yolks, 220g caster sugar, 4g gelatine

Place all of the ingredients, except the gelatine, into the Thermomix. Put the machine on Varoma Cook setting and programme to 100°C for 8 minutes. Once cooked, place in a bowl and add the bloomed gelatine. Pass through a fine chinois and leave to cool. Bag ready for use once cold.

YOGHURT MERINGUES

100g egg whites, 200g caster sugar, 5g yoghurt powder, 15g lemon yoghurt

Whisk the egg whites on a mixing machine on a high speed, add the sugar in two stages, once the meringue is stiff peak add the yoghurt powder. Pipe into think sticks, sprinkle with lemon yoghurt and dry in an oven at 70c for 4 hours.

LEMON YOGHURT POWDER

50g yoghurt powder, 10g lemon zest, 2g lemon juice, 1g yellow Sevarome colour

Blend all of ingredients together in a Thermomix. Sprinkle onto a silicone mat and dry, either in a dehydrator over night or in an oven at 65°C for 8 hours.

LEMON CONFIT

50g blanched lemon strips, 100g water, 125g caster sugar, 30g glucose, 10g fresh lemon juice

Blanch the lemon strips 5 times to remove the bitterness from the lemon. Bring the water, castor sugar, glucose and lemon juice to the boil, add the lemon strips and cook to 105°C. Leave to cool in the syrup, use at garnish.

LEMON CREMEUX

200g whole milk, 8g lemon zest, 50g caster sugar, 12g custard powder, 30g egg yolks, 3g gelatine, 3g fresh lemon juice, 125g butter

Bring the milk and lemon zest to the boil. Whisk together the yolks, sugar and custard powder. Pour the lemon milk through a fine chinois over over the yolk mix and return to the heat. Cook the mix until boiling, whisking constantly, remove from the heat and add the bloomed gelatine. Place into a Thermomix and at low speed add the butter, then the fresh lemon juice. Mix until emulsified. Bag ready to use and refrigerate

YOGHURT NUGGETS

55g maltosec, 20g lemon oil, 10g non acidic yoghurt powder, 5g acidic yoghurt powder

Whisk everything together to form yoghurt nuggets. Bag ready to use.

Deconstructed Desserts

Apple Pie And Custard

VANILLA SHORTCRUST TART

200g T55 soft flour, 30g corn starch, 70g icing sugar, 20g egg yolks, 205g butter, 2g salt, 2 Bourbon vanilla pods

Cream the butter and the icing sugar on a mixing machine with a paddle. Sieve the cornstarch, salt and flour together. Add the egg yolks and vanilla pod seeds and mix to a smooth paste. Finally add the dry ingredients and work to a dough. Clingfilm and refrigerate for one hour. Roll the pastry to 1cm depth and line a small tart case. Blind bake at 165°C for 10 minutes. Remove the beans and bake again at 170°C for 5 minutes. Leave to cool.

APPLE COMPOTE AND PUREE

100g Bramley apples, 1g cinnamon, 10g caster sugar, 2g lemon juice

Peel, core and dice the apples. Place in a large pan with the remaining ingredients. Cook on a medium heat until the apples are soft but still have texture. Blitz some with a hand blender into a compote. Leave to chill and then bag the compote ready for use. For the purée, place the rest into a Thermomix and blend until a smooth paste is formed. Pass through a fine chinois and chill.

CREME PATISSERIE

125g whole milk, 1 Tahiti vanilla pod, 30g caster sugar, 10g custard powder, 20g egg yolks

Bring the milk and vanilla seeds and pod to the boil. Whisk the sugar, yolks and custard powder. Pass the vanilla milk through a fine chinois over the egg mix and return to the heat. Cook again until boiling, whisking constantly. Spread onto a silicone mat to cool. Clingfilm to touch. Once cold, place in a Thermomix and blitz until smooth, ready to pipe into the tart shells.

CRUMBLE NUGGETS

125g unsalted butter, 125g demerara sugar, 187g T55 soft flour, 67g ground almonds, 2g lemon zest, 1g ground cinnamon

Place all of the ingredients into a mixing machine with a paddle, beat together until a crumble is formed. Sprinkle the nuggets onto a tray mat and bake at 165°C for 12 minutes. Leave to cool.

AERATED APPLE JELLY

125g fresh Bramley apple juice, 20g caster sugar, 5g gelatine

Place a mixing machine bowl and whisk in the freezer 1 hour prior to use. Bring the juice and sugar to the boil, add the bloomed gelatine and stir well. Pass through a muslin cloth and cool on an ice bath until set. Once set, place in the mixing machine bowl and whisk on a high speed until the jelly is aerated and doubled in volume. Pipe into moulds and freeze.

APPLE GLAZE

250g fresh Bramley juice, 125g clear neutral glaze, 0.2g pistachio green colour, 10g gelatine

Bring the juice, glaze and colour to the boil. Once boiling add the bloomed gelatine and pass through a muslin cloth. Chill the mix then use at 18°C to glaze the aerated jellies.

CARAMELISED APPLES

100g Bramley apple juice, 2 Granny Smith apples, 200g caster sugar

Peel and core the apples. Make small scoops of the apple using a prism scoop. Make a direct caramel with the sugar. Once a dark golden brown colour, add the apples and cook until evenly coloured and coated in the caramel. Deglaze with the Bramley apple juice. Drain and leave to cool.

Deconstructed Desserts

Pina Colada Rum Baba

BABA DOUGH

120g strong Ffour, 60g whole milk, 8g yeast, 75g whole eggs, 12g caster sugar, 2g salt, 40g softened unsalted butter

Using the dough hook, place the flour, sugar and salt in a mixing machine on speed no.1. Warm the milk to 28°C and add the fresh yeast, leave to dissolve then stir. Add the eggs to the dough, followed by the yeast milk, and mix for a few minutes to a smooth dough. Place the dough in a bowl and leave to prove at 29°C, clingfilm to touch and place a cloth on top. Once doubled in size, place the dough back into the machine. Add the softened butter, gradually. Mix in the machine until all the butter has been absorbed into the dough. Pipe the mix into the moulds and leave to prove again at 29°C. Once the dough has risen bake at 200°C for 5 minutes. Turn down the oven at bake at 170°C for a further 10 minutes. Once cool remove from moulds.

SOAKING SYRUP

200g fresh pineapple juice, 50g Malibu, 100g Havana mum, 2g fresh mint, 300g caster sugar,100g water

Bring everything to the boil, reduce the syrup and cook to 40 Brix with a refractometer. Soak the baked baba in the syrup for 6 minutes, turning evenly.

PINA COLADA MOUSSE

200g pineapple purée reduced, 50g coconut milk, 30g egg yolks, 10g castor sugar, 5g Malibu, 4g gelatine, 10g egg whites, 20g caster sugar, 5g water, 120g whipping cream

Reduce the pineapple purée with the malibu to 50g. Once reduced add the coconut milk and bring the boil. Whisk the yolks and castor sugar. Pour the liquid over the yolk mix. Return to the heat and cook to 75°C. Add the bloomed gelatine and stir well. Pass through a fine chinois and chill base to 25°C. Make an Italian meringue with the whites, sugar and water. Once stiff peak fold meringue into the base.Whisk the cream to ribbon stage and fold through the mix last. Pipe into moulds to set.

PINEAPPLE CARAMEL

100g caster sugar, 140g fresh pineapple juice, 20g Malibu, 3g lime zest, 10g lime juice

Make a direct caramel add the sugar in 3 stages until golden brown. Deglaze with the pineapple juice, Malibu, lime zest and juice. Bring back to the boil and reduce. Cook to 46 Brix with a refractometer.

COCONUT LIME FLUID GEL

100g coconut milk, 2g lime juice, 1.2g agar agar, 3g caster sugar

Mix the sugar and agar agar together. Bring the coconut milk and lime juice to the boil. Gradually pour in the sugar mix whisking constantly and bring back to the boil. Pour onto a silicone mat to set. Once set Place in a Thermomix and blend to a smooth paste.bag ready for use.

PINEAPPLE POACHING LIQUOR

1 whole pineapple juice, 20g Malibu, 2 star anise, 1 cinnamon stick, 10g lime juice, 8g lime zest

Juice the pineapple, place the star anise and cinnamon in a pan roast on a dry heat.

Add the pineapple juice, lime zest, juice and malibu. Bring everything to the boil, leave to cool. Once cold vacumn pack till airtight. Use as required.

PRESSED PINEAPPLE
100g pineapple poaching liquo, 30g pineapple

Peel the pineapple and cut into 2cm dice. Place in a vacuum pack bag with the liquid and seal until airtight. Leave for 12 hours to macerate. To use, drain from the liquid.

Entremets

67

Tropical

Entremets 69

70 Entremets

COCONUT LIME SPONGE

200g whole eggs, 300g caster sugar, 150g whipping cream, 200g T55 soft flour, 80g desiccated coconut, 5g baking powder, 100g unsalted butter, 10g lime zest

Whisk the whole eggs and sugar to a thick cold sabayon, add the sugar gradually in two stages. Once at ribbon stage, pour in the whipping cream, then pour in the warm melted butter and lime zest. Fold in the sieved flour, coconut and baking powder. Spread onto a silicone baking mat. Bake at 155°C for 10 minutes and then 165°C for 6 minutes. Take out of the oven and soak with the lime syrup. (see below)

LIME SYRUP

300g caster sugar, 150g water, 150g lime juice, 20g lime zest

Bring everything to the boil and cook with the refractometer to 48 Brix. Use the syrup to soak the sponge.

COCONUT PASSIONFRUIT BRULEE INSERT

330g coconut milk, 45g passionfruit purée, 50g whole eggs, 75g egg yolks, 70g caster sugar, 10g Malibu rum, 6g gelatine

Bring the coconut milk, malibu and passionfruit purée to the boil. Whisk together the whole eggs, egg yolks and sugar. Pour the boiling liquid over the egg mix, pass through a fine chinois. Place in a tray and bake at 90°C for 25 minutes until set. Remove from the tray and place the set brulee mix into a bowl, add the bloomed gelatine and whisk well. Leave to cool to 30°C then pour into an entremet mould to set.

PINEAPPLE AERATED MERINGUE INSERT

250g pineapple purée, 10g Malibu, 12g gelatine, 50g egg whites, 90g caster sugar, 40g yoghurt crispies

Bring the pineapple purée and Malibu to the boil, add the bloomed gelatine and stir well. Leave mix to cool to 20°C. Make an italian Meringue, once cool fold into pineapple base. Fold through the crispies, then pipe into entremet mould and freeze.

ALPHONSO MANGO MOUSSE

250g Alphonso mango purée reduced to 200g, 10g whole milk, 60g egg yolks, 6g gelatine, 200g whipping cream, 25g egg whites, 50g caster sugar, 20g water

Reduce the purée, with the milk, to 200g. Whisk the egg yolks well then pour the purée over the yolks. Return to the pan and cook to 75°C stirring constantly. Add the bloomed gelatine and whisk well. Leave mix to chill to 25°C. Whip the cream to soft peak stage. Make an italian meringue with the remaining ingredients. Once cool, fold into the mango base then fold in the whipped cream last. Pipe into entremet mould.

YELLOW SPRAY

250g zephyr white chocolate, 100g cocoa butter, 25g yellow colour

Melt the white chocolate to 45°C. Melt the cocoa butter, add the colour and stir well. Add to the chocolate and pass through a muslin cloth. Use at 35°C to spray the cake.

72 Entremets

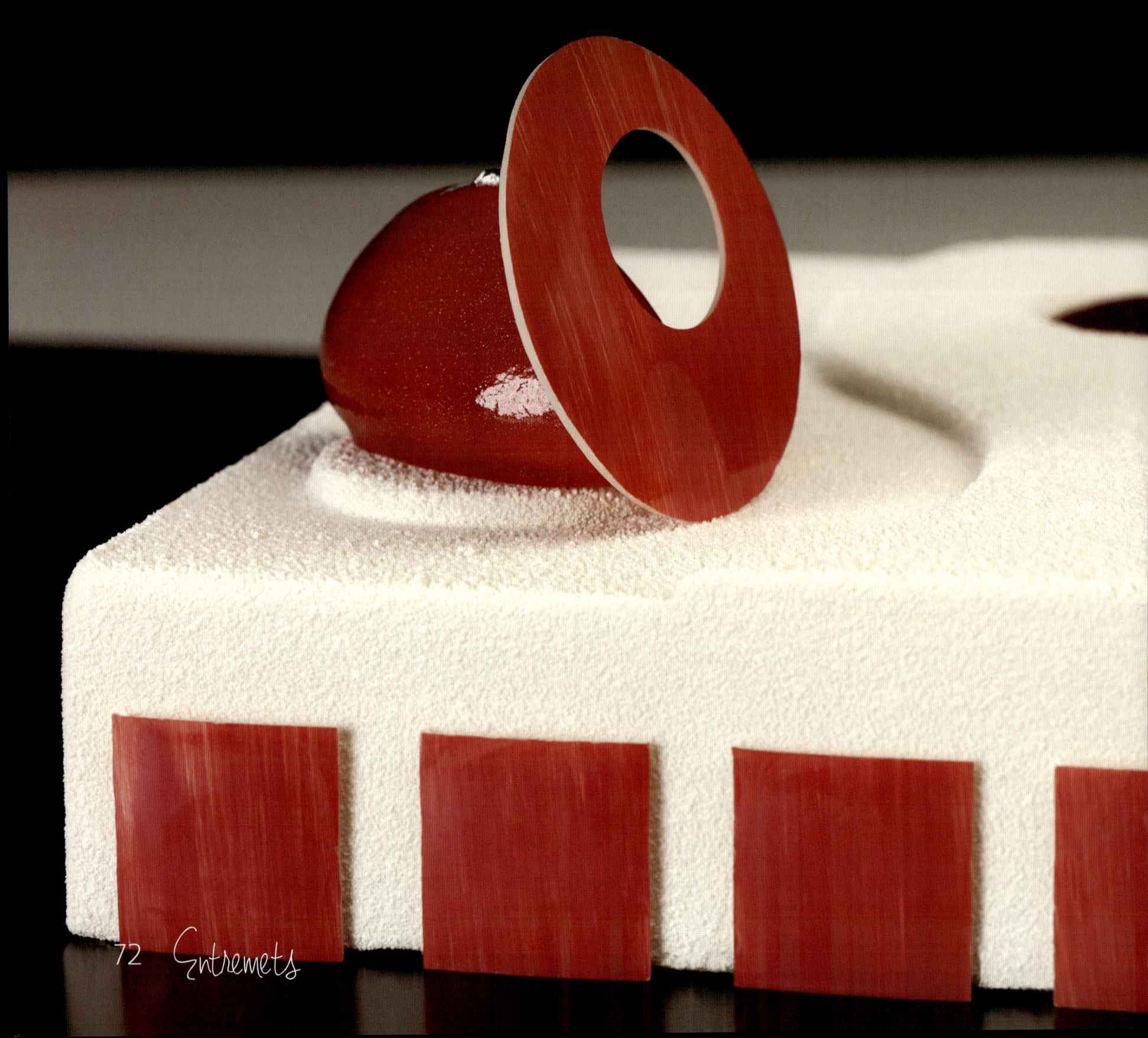

Strawberries & Cream

Entremets 73

ALMOND PAIN DE GENE

140g unsalted butter, 110g caster sugar, 140g ground almonds, 25g T55 soft flour, 25g cornflour, 200g whole eggs, Tempered white chocolate

Cream the butter and the castor sugar in a mixing machine, with the paddle attachment. Add 80g of the whole eggs and mix well. Add the remaining dry ingredients and mix again. Finally add the remaining 120g whole eggs and mix to a smooth paste. Spread into a silicone sheet and bake at 165°C for 12 minutes. Once cold, cut the sheet into two discs and spread tempered, white chocolate onto the bottom disc.

STRAWBERRY JAM

300g fresh strawberries, 40g pectin jam sugar, 3g citric acid

Cut the fresh strawberries into quarters, add the pectin sugar and citric acid. Cook to 62° Brix using a refractometer. Spread onto a tray to cool. Once cold and set, spread between the two pain de gene sheets to sandwich.

LEMON CURD INSERT

150g lemon juice, 160g unsalted butter, 200g whole eggs, 50g egg yolks, 200g caster sugar, 4g lemon zest, 3g gelatine

Place all of the ingredients, except the gelatine, into a Thermomix. Place on Varoma and set to the 100° cook cycle for 8 minutes. Once cooked, pass through a fine chinois. Place into a bowl and add the bloomed gelatine, stirring well. Chill mix to 22°C then pipe into entremet mould to set.

YOGHURT VANILLA MOUSSE INSERT

160g caster sugar, 80g egg yolks, 15g whole egg, 550g Greek yoghurt, 420g whipping cream, 20g gelatine, 3 Tahiti vanilla pods

Make a pâte à bombe with the whole egg, yolks and sugar. Once you have add the cooked sugar syrup, add the vanilla pods seeds and whisk until cool. Take 80g of the whipping cream and bring to the boil. Once boiling and add the bloomed gelatine. Whip the remaining cream to soft peak stage. Fold the Gelatine cream mix into the pâte à bombe. Fold the pâte à bombe into the yoghurt and stir well. Fold through the whipped cream and pipe into moulds.

STRAWBERRY CREAM

250g wild strawberry purée, 60g egg yolks, 2g strawberry Sevarome colour, 6g gelatine, 200g whipping cream, 25g egg whites, 50g caster sugar

Bring the purée to the boil, whisk the egg yolks. Pour the purée over the yolks, return to the heat and cook the mixture to 75°C. Add the bloomed gelatine and colour then chill to 25°C. Whip the cream to ribbon stage and reserve. Use the remaining ingredients to make an Italian meringue. Fold the meringue through the chilled base and add the cream last. Stir well and pipe into mould to set.

WHIPPED VANILLA GEL

250g whole milk, 20g whipping cream, 6 Tahiti vanilla pods, 26g gelatine, 20g egg whites, 40g caster sugar

Place the mixing machine bowl and whisk in the freezer 3 hours prior to use. Bring the milk, cream and vanilla to the boil, add the bloomed gelatine and stir well, then chill to 5°C. Place into the mixing machine and whisk on full speed, until the mix is fully aerated and doubled in volume. Make an Italian meringue with the egg whites and sugar and fold through jelly mix. Pipe into quenelle moulds and freeze.

CHOCOLATE SPRAY MIX

300g Zephyr white chocolate, 140g cocoa butter, 20g white colour powder

Melt the chocolate to 45°C. Melt the cocoa butter to 40°C, add the white colour and whisk well. Mix together with the chocolate and pass through a muslin cloth. Place into a spray gun and use at 35°C.

Pistachio & Apricot Gateau

PISTACHIO DACQUOISE

200g ground pistachios, 200g ground almonds, 200g icing sugar, 250g egg whites, 75g caster sugar

Whisk the egg whites with the caster sugar, adding the sugar in two stages. Sieve together the icing sugar, ground almonds and ground pistachio nuts. Once the meringue is stiff peak, fold through the nuts and icing sugar mix in three stages. Spread onto a silicone mat and bake at 165°C for 14 minutes. Cut into required rectangle once cool.

APRICOT JELLY INSERT

225g apricot purée, 6.5g gelatine, 30g caster sugar, 50g roasted diced apricots, 10g honey, 1 cinnamon stick.

Cut the apricots in half, place on a tray and drizzle with honey and a cinnamon stick. Cover with foil and bake at 170°C for 15 minutes. Once cold, remove the skin and cut into 1cm dice. Bring the purée and sugar to the boil, add the bloomed gelatine and mix well. Fold through the diced apricot and leave to cool on an ice bath. Once set, place the mix into the mould to set.

PISTACHIO BRULEE INSERT

160g whipping cream, 100g pistachio paste, 50g whole eggs, 45g egg yolks, 25g caster sugar, 4g gelatine

Entremets 77

Bring the cream and pistachio paste to the boil. Whisk the whole eggs, yolks and caster sugar. Pour the hot pistachio cream over the egg mix and whisk well. Place in a tray and bake at 90°C for 25 minutes. Once cooked, pass the mix through a fine chinois into a bowl, add the bloomed gelatine and whisk well. Leave the mixture to chill to 20°C then pipe into mould to set.

APRICOT MOUSSE

400g apricot purée reduced to 200g, 80g egg yolks, 25g whole eggs, 10g whole milk, 8g gelatine, 200g whipping cream, 100g caster sugar

Reduce the purée, make a pâte à bombe with the whole eggs, yolks and sugar. Once the sugar syrup has reached soft ball stage (121°C) add the bloomed gelatine to the syrup and stir well, pour this over the egg mix and whisk in the mixing machine. Separately whisk the cream to ribbon stage. Fold the pâte à bombe into the purée mix and then fold in the whipped cream. Pipe into moulds and set.

APRICOT SPRAY GEL

250g apricot purée, 50g stock syrup, one to one, 4g pectin NH, 10g caster sugar

Bring the purée and stock syrup the boil. Mix the sugar and pectin together and gradually add to the boiling purée solution, whisking, and bring back to the boil. Pass through a fine chinois. Place in spray gun and spray 30°C.

PISTACHIO CREMEUX

200g whole milk, 100g pistachio paste, 30g egg yolks, 20g caster sugar, 12g custard powder, 3g gelatine, 125g butter

Bring the whole milk to the boil. Whisk together the egg yolks, caster sugar and custard powder. Pour the hot milk over the egg mix and whisk. Return to the heat, bring back to the boil, whisking constantly. Add the bloomed gelatine and stir. Place in a Thermomix. At low speed, add the pistachio pate and the diced butter. Mix for several minutes until the creméux is emulsified.

PISTACHIO PASTE

200g whole pistachio nuts, 30g ground nut oil

Warm the nuts in the oven at 120°C for 10 minutes. Place in a Thermomix with the oil and, on a high speed, blend to a smooth paste. Bag ready for use.

Entremets 79

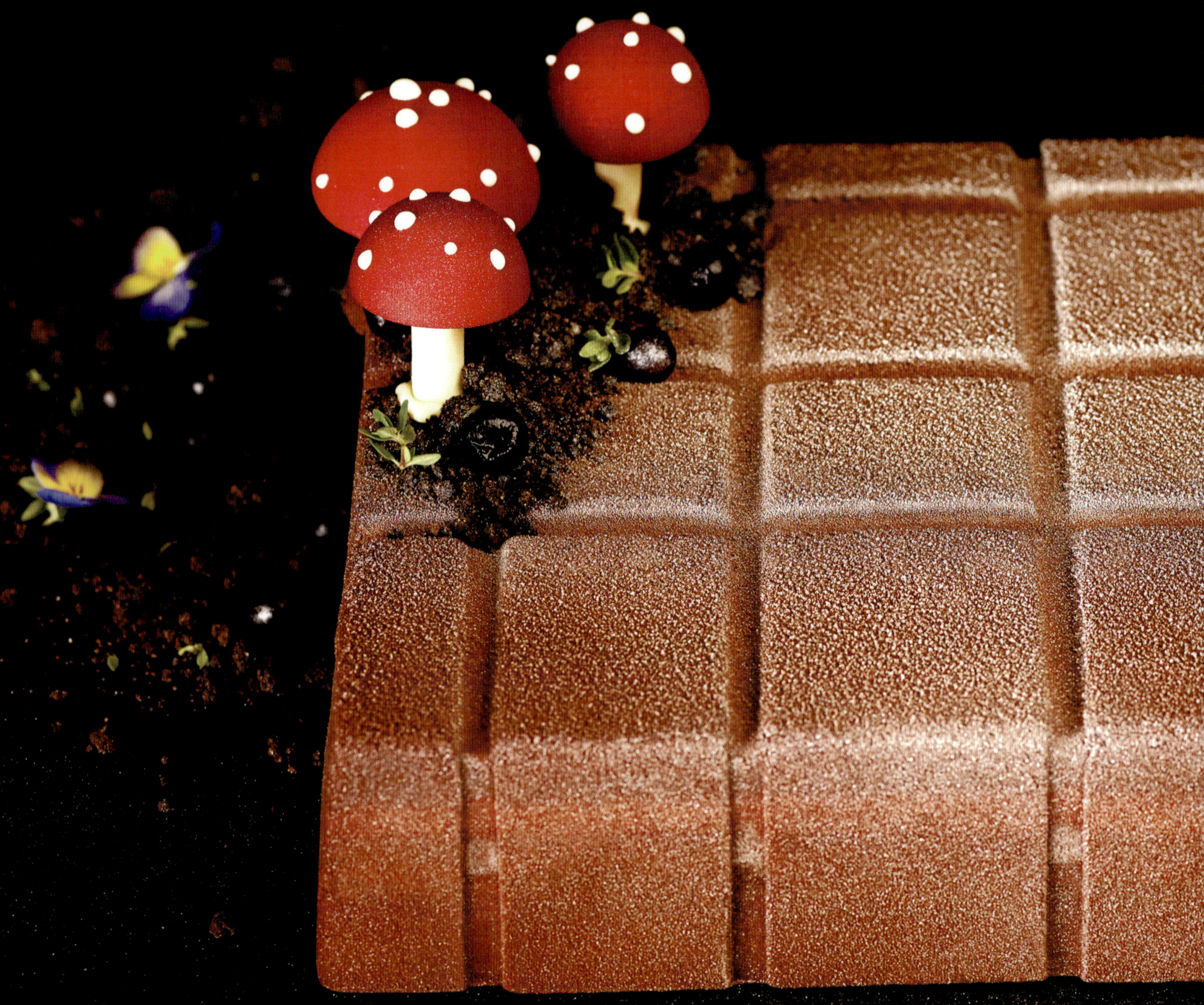

Woodland Forest

Entremets 81

CHOCOLATE SACHER SANDWICH

300g Alto el Sol 65% dark chocolate, 260g unsalted butter, 260g ground almonds, 160g egg yolks, 70g T55 soft flour, 240g egg whites, 260g caster sugar, 80g Alto El Sol 65% for tempering

Melt the 300g of chocolate to 40°C. Melt the butter to 35°C. Mix the two together. Make a french meringue in the mixing machine with the whites and caster sugar, adding the sugar in three stages until the meringue is at stiff peak stage. Add the egg yolks to the chocolate butter mixture and whisk well. On a low speed, add the chocolate mixture to the meringue to form a chocolate meringue. Sieve together the ground almonds and the flour and gradually fold this into the chocolate meringue. Once mixed, spread onto a silicone mat and bake at 165°C for 8 minutes. When cooled, cut into two discs. Temper dark chocolate and spread thinly onto the bottom disc.

BLACKCURRANT VIOLET JAM

150g blackcurrants, 30g pectin jam sugar, 5g blitzed violets, 1g citric acid.

Place all of the ingredients into a pan and cook to 62° Brix with refractometer. Leave to cool. Sandwich the jam between to the two Sacher discs.

VIOLET CREAM

65g whole milk, 65g whipping cream, 30g egg yolks, 40g caster sugar, 3g violet essence, 3g gelatine, 150g whipping cream

Bring the milk and cream to the boil, whisk the egg yolks and sugar. Pour the liquid over the yolk mix, return to the heat and cook to 75°C. Add the bloomed gelatine and violet essence and stir well. Pass through a fine chinois and leave base to cool to 20°C. Whip the cream to soft peak and fold into base. Pipe into mould to set.

LEMON THYME MOUSSELINE

200g milk, 15g picked lemon thyme, 2g lemon zest, 30g egg yolks, 20g caster sugar, 12g custard powder, 180g butter

Bring the milk, lemon thyme and zest to the boil, clingfilm and leave to infuse for 40 minutes. Whisk the egg yolks, caster sugar and custard powder together. Bring the milk back to the boil then pour through a fine chinois over the egg mix, and whisking well. Return to the heat and continue to cook until the mix is boiling. Place in a bowl and leave to cool with, clingfilm touching the surface to prevent a skin forming. Once this base is at 3°C, gradually whisk in the softened butter. Once emulsified pipe into moulds to set.

BLACKCURRANT JELLY

225g blackcurrant purée, 7g gelatine, 1g citric acid, 30g whole milk

Bring the whole milk and purée to the boil with the acid, add the bloomed gelatine and stir well. Leave to cool. Once at 20°C pipe into moulds to set.

CHOCOLATE BLACKCURRANT MOUSSE

280g Madirofolo 65% chocolate, 90g caster sugar, 30g water, 45g whole eggs, 35g egg yolks, 12g gelatine, 225g blackcurrant purée, 280g whipping cream

Melt the chocolate to 40°C. Make a pâte à bombe with the whole eggs, yolks and sugar syrup, cooking the syrup to soft boil. Bring the purée to the boil, add the bloomed gelatine to this and stir well. Whip the cream to ribbon stage. Fold the purée into the pate bombe, add the melted chocolate and mix with a spatula. Finally fold through the whipped cream. Pipe the mousse into moulds to set.

CHOCOLATE SPRAY

150g Madirofolo, 65% dark chocolate, 75g cocoa butter, 2g gold shimmer

Melt the chocolate to 40°C. Melt the cocoa butter to 45°C and add the shimmer to the cocoa butter. Mix together and pass through a muslin cloth. Place in spray gun and use at 35°C.

Chocolate Tonka Praline

Entremets 85

CHOCOLATE BROWNIE SHEETS

125g whole eggs, 180g caster sugar, 144g unsalted melted butter, 72g T55 soft flour, 144g Cuba 70% dark chocolate, 72g Saint Domingue 70% chopped dark chocolate, 72g roasted chopped hazelnuts, 80g Saint, Domingue 70% tempered chocolate

Whisk the eggs and sugar to a thick cold sabayon, in a mixing machine, adding the caster sugar in three stages until stiff peaks. Melt the chocolate to 40°C. Melt the butter to 35°C. Mix together. Sieve the flour. Fold the chocolate butter mix into the sabayon by hand with a spatula. Fold in the sieved flour and finally the chopped chocolate and hazelnuts. Spread onto a silicone mat and bake at 165°C for 10 minutes. Once cool, cut out a heart disc and spread the bottom with a thin layer of the tempered chocolate.

HAZELNUT FEUILLETINE

150g hazelnut paste, 40g feuilletine, 80g Papouasie 35.8% milk chocolate

Melt the milk chocolate to 45°C. Add the feuilletine and hazelnut paste and stir well. Spread between two sheets of silicone paper and roll to 1cm depth. Leave to set. Once crystallised, cut out a heart disc and sit on top of the brownie.

HAZELNUT PASTE

150g roasted hazelnuts, 20g hazelnut oil

Roast the hazelnut on a tray at 175°C for 10 minutes until golden brown. Place in a Thermomix with the oil and blend on a high speed until a smooth paste. Bag ready for use.

TONKA BEAN MOUSSE

100g whole milk, 120g whipping cream, 8g blitzed Tonka beans, 63g egg yolks, 20g caster sugar, 375g Papouasie, 35.8% milk chocolate, 375g whipping cream, 9g gelatine

Bring the cream and milk to the boil, add the blitzed Tonka beans. Clingfilm the pan and leave to infuse for 25 minutes. Whisk the yolks and sugar, bring the Tonka cream back to the boil, pour directly over the yolks, whisk well. Return to the heat and cook to 75°C, stirring constantly. Once at 75°C, add the bloomed gelatine. Melt the chocolate to 40°C. Pass the mix through a fine chinois over the chocolate, and stir with a spatula. Leave base to cool to 25°C. Whip the cream to ribbon stage, fold the cream into the base and pipe into moulds to set.

HAZELNUT PRALINE

300g roasted hazelnuts, 150g caster sugar, 20g glucose, 70g water

Place the sugar, water and glucose in a pan and cook to 121°C. Warm the roasted nuts in the oven at 120°C. Add the nuts to the sugar and stir constantly until the sugar caramelises. Once all the nuts are coated and golden brown spread onto a silicone tray to cool. Once cool break into small pieces. Place the nuts into the Thermomix and grind to a paste on a low speed. Bag ready for use.

HAZELNUT CREMEUX

220g whole milk, 100g hazelnut praline, 30g egg yolks, 10g caster sugar, 12g custard powder, 3g gelatine, 125g unsalted butter

Bring the milk to the boil. Whisk the yolks, caster sugar and custard powder. Pour the boiling milk over the egg milk and whisk. Return to the heat and cook until mix is boiling, stirring constantly. Add the bloomed gelatine and mix with a spatula. Place in a Thermomix and, on a low speed, add the paste and the butter. Mix for several minutes until emulsified. Pipe into moulds to set.

DARK CHOCOLATE MOUSSE

285g Saint Domingue 70% dark chocolate, 110g caster sugar, 35g water, 45g whole eggs, 38g egg yolks, 8g gelatine, 150g hazelnut paste, 290g whipping cream

Melt the chocolate to 40°C. Make a pâte à bombe with the sugar, water, yolks and whole eggs. Once the sugar syrup is at 121°C, add the bloomed gelatine, stir well and pour over the egg mix. Whisk in the mixing machine until at stiff peak stage. Whip the cream to ribbon stage. Pour the hazelnut paste into the pâte à bombe, fold through the melted chocolate, finally fold in the whipping cream. Pour into the moulds and set.

Peanut Caramel Aztec

Entremets 89

90 Entremets

SEA SALT CARAMEL

150g caster sugar, 30g glucose, 150g whipping cream, 1 Tahiti vanilla pod, 3g sea salt, 15g unsalted butter

Bring the cream to the boil with the vanilla pod, seeds and salt. Make a direct caramel, gradually adding the sugar in 6 stages until a clear caramel brown, then add the glucose and the butter, stir until emulsified. Add the cream in three stages stirring well each time. Bring back to the boil and reduce by half. Pass through a fine chinois and leave to cool.

CHOCOLATE FLOURLESS SPONGE

135g Tanzanie 75% chocolate, 36g unsalted butter, 36g caster sugar, 150g egg whites, 50g egg yolks, 14g cocoa powder, 80g Tanzanie 75% chocolate, tempered

Melt the chocolate to 45°C. Melt the butter to 35°C. Make a French meringue with the egg whites and sugar. Mix the chocolate and butter together, add the yolks to this mix, fold into the French meringue. Sieve the cocoa powder and fold in last. Spread onto a silicone mat and bake at 170°C for 6 minutes. Cut two discs. Spread the bottom of one of the discs with the tempered chocolate.

PEANUT CARAMEL

150g sea salt caramel, 70g chopped roasted salted peanuts

Mix both ingredients together with a spatula.

PEANUT PASTE

150g roasted salted peanuts, 30g peanut oil

Roast the salted peanuts at 175°C for 10 minutes. Place in a Thermomix with the oil and blend to a smooth paste. Bag ready for use.

PEANUT MOUSSE

150g whole milk, 150g whipping cream, 84g egg yolks, 42g caster sugar, 90g Zephyr 34% white chocolate, 250g peanut paste, 450g whipping cream, 5g gelatine

Make an Anglaise with the whole milk, whipping cream, yolks and sugar, cook to 75°C. Add the bloomed gelatine and stir well. Pour the Anglaise through a fine chinois over the melted white chocolate. Add the peanut paste. Chill this base to 25°C. Whip the cream to soft peak stage and fold into the base. Pipe into moulds and set.

MILK CHOCOLATE MOUSSE

100g whole milk, 100g whipping cream, 65g egg yolks, 10g whole egg, 90g caster sugar, 25g water, 375g Alunga 41% chocolate, 375g whipping cream, 9g gelatine

Melt the chocolate to 40°C. Bring the milk and cream to the boil and pour over the melted chocolate. Make a pâte à bombe with the sugar, water, yolks and whole egg. Once the sugar syrup is at 121°C, add the bloomed gelatine, stir well and add to the whisked yolks.

Continue to whisk until stiff peaks. Whip the cream to ribbon stage. Fold the pâte à bombe into the chocolate mix, then fold through the whipped cream. Pipe into moulds and set.

CHOCOLATE SPRAY

250g milk chocolate, 125g cocoa butter, 10g gold shimmer powder

Melt the chocolate to 45°C. Melt the cocoa butter, add the shimmer to the cocoa butter and stir well. Mix with the chocolate. Pass the mix through muslin cloth. Use at 35°C to spray the cake.

Small Sweets

93

94 *Small Sweets*

Nougat De Montelimar

NOUGAT DE MONTELIMAR

275g flaked almonds, 275g chopped hazelnuts, 50g whole pistachio, 200g water, 640g castor sugar, 180g glucose, 80g egg whites, 32g caster sugar, 180g honey

Roast the almonds and the hazelnuts at 170°C until golden brown. Turn the temperature down to 120°C add the pistachios and keep all the nuts warm. Boil the 640g of sugar with the water to 156°C. When the sugar has reached 135°C, warm the honey. Whisk the whites with the 32g of sugar then add the warmed honey, followed by the boiling sugar syrup. Whisk for two minutes on high speed until a stiff meringue. Add the nuts and mix for a further minute. Spread onto a tray lined with rice paper, flatten with a palette knife. Once set cut into small squares 2cm by 2cm.

96 *Small Sweets*

Yuzu & Lime Pate D' Fruit

195g yuzu juice, 1g lime zest, 5g lime juice 4.8g yellow pectin, 150g caster sugar, 38g inverted sugar, 3g citric acid, 2g water

Bring the yuzu juice, lime juice and zest to the boil. Mix the pectin and sugar together. Gradually add this to the boiling liquid, add the inverted sugar. Cook this to 105°C, then add the citric acid and water. Pour immediately into the moulds and leave to set. Once set and cold, roll in granulated sugar.

Pate D' Fruit

200g raspberry purée, 80g caster sugar, 5.5g yellow pectin, 30g glucose, 10g raspberry sherbet, 2g citric acid

Bring the purée to the boil, mix the pectin and sugar together. Add the glucose to the purée and boil until dissolved. Gradually pour in the pectin sugar mix and whisk well. Cook to 105°C, add the citric acid and raspberry sherbet and stir. Pour into moulds to set. Once set and cold roll in raspberry sherbet and granulated sugar.

Apple Calvados Pate D' Fruit

400g Bramley apple juice, 35g Calvados, 70g caster sugar, 3g yellow pectin, 30g glucose, 2g citric acid, 2g water

Reduce the apple juice to 200g, once reduced add the calvados and glucose and boil until dissolved. Mix the pectin and the sugar together. Gradually pour the pectin sugar mix into liquid and whisk well. Cook to 105°C, add the citric acid and water then pour into moulds to set. Once set and cold roll in granulated sugar.

100 Small Sweets

Blood Orange Turkish Delight

200g caster sugar, 60g blood orange purée, 2g blood orange zest, 45g water, 23g cornflour, 8g gelatine, 2g cream of tartar

Bring the purée, sugar and zest to the boil. Whisk together the water and cornflour and add to the boiled purée mix. Once the liquid is 110°C, add the cream of tartar and gelatine. Pour the mix into a tray lined with acetate and leave to set. Once set cut into 3cm cubes and roll in a 50/50 mix of icing sugar and cornflour.

102 Small Sweets

Mini Macarons

The Amond Base and Italian Meringue recipes below form the base mixture for all of the macarons in this section. You simply need to add the various colours or flavours at the appropriate time and sandwich together the macarons with the corresponding fillings.

Basic Macaron Recipe

ALMOND BASE

300g ground almonds, 300g icing sugar, 110g egg whites

Place the icing sugar, almonds and egg whites into a mixing bowl with the paddle attachment. Mix on a medium speed for several minutes until a smooth paste is formed.

ITALIAN MERINGUE

110g egg whites, 10g castor sugar, 300g caster sugar, 65g water

Place the egg whites in a mixing machine with the 10g of caster sugar. Place the sugar and water in a pan, cook to 121°C, then slowly pour over the whisking whites on a slow speed. At this stage add the required colours. Once the meringue is cooked, at stiff peak stage, take half of the meringue and mix into the almond base, mix this till smooth. Finally fold in the remaining meringue and mix until the base is flowing. You can now pipe the macaron mix. Once piped, leave to dry on a silicone mat for 20 minutes until a skin is formed on top of the macarons. Bake at 130°C for 16 minutes. Once cold remove from the mat, pair and fill.

VARIATIONS:

Spiced Ginger Bread Macarons

MACARON

1 batch basic macaron mix, 4g brown Sevarome colour, 30g blitzed dried gingerbread

Make the basic mixture as per the recipe, adding the 30g of blitzed dried gingerbread to the almond base before adding meringue. Add the colouring to the meringue before mixing with almond base, then pipe and bake as instructed.

SPICED GINGERBREAD GANACHE

80g blitzed gingerbread nuggets (see page...), 220g whipping cream, 250g Biskella milk chocolate, 25g inverted sugar, 90g unsalted butter, 1g Malden sea salt, 2g mixed spice, 2g ground cinnamon, 2g ground ginger

Bring the cream, ginger, cinnamon, mixed spice and salt to the boil. Remove from the heat, cling film the pan and leave to infuse for 20 minutes. Melt the chocolate to 40°C. Add the inverted sugar to the chocolate. Bring the cream back to the boil. Add to the chocolate in 3 stages, mix until smooth and glossy. Place in a Thermomix on a low speed and gradually add the butter until the ganache is emulsified. Place the ganache in a bowl to cool. Once at 18°C, fold through the blitzed gingerbread nuggets. Bag the ganache ready for use and store at 12°C. Use to sandwich the cooked macarons when needed.

Mint & Lemon Macarons

MACARON

1 batch basic macaron mix, 2g yellow colour, 2g green colour, 10g lemon zest

Make the basic mixture as per the recipe, adding the lemon zest to macaron base before adding the meringue. Divide this mix into two before adding the colours, one half green and one half yellow, then pipe and bake as instructed.

MINT LEMON GANACHE

10g fresh mint, 170g whipping cream, 2g lemon zest, 285g Opayls 33% white chocolate, 15g inverted sugar, 50g unsalted butter, 10g lemon confit pieces (0.5cm dice)

Bring the cream to the boil, place in a Thermomix and add the fresh mint and lemon zest. Blend of full speed for 8 minutes. Pass the cream through a muslin cloth. Melt the chocolate to 40°C, add the inverted sugar. Bring the mint cream back to the boil. Add to the chocolate in 3 stages, mix until smooth and glossy.

Place in a Thermomix on a low speed and gradually add the butter until the ganache is emulsified. Place the ganache in a bowl to cool. Once at 18°C, add the diced lemon confit. Bag the ganache ready to use and store at 12°C. Use to sandwich the macarons when needed.

Jasmine Tea Cremeux

MACARON

210g whole milk, 4g jasmine tea blitzed, 30g egg yolks, 25g caster sugar, 12g custard powder, 3g gelatine, 125g unsalted butter

Make the basic mixture as per the recipe, adding the 30g of blitzed jasmine tea to the almond base before adding meringue. Add the colouring to the meringue before mixing with almond base, then pipe and bake as instructed.

JASMINE TEA CREMEUX

Bring the whole milk to the boil, remove from the heat, add the tea, cling film the pan and leave to infuse for 25 minutes. Bring back to the boil and pass through a muslin cloth. Whisk the yolks, sugar and custard powder. Pout the boiled liquid over the egg mix and return the heat, cook the mix until boiling whisking constantly. Remove from the heat and add the bloomed gelatine, stir well. Place in a bowl and blend with a hand blender, gradually add the butter until emulsified. Bag and refrigerate ready for use.

Spiced Pumpkin Macarons

MACARON

1 batch basic macaron mix, 2g orange colour, 2g ground star anise, 3g ground cinnamon, 2g mixed spice

Make the basic mixture as per the recipe, adding the spices to the almond base before adding meringue. Add the colouring to the meringue before mixing with almond base, then pipe and bake as instructed.

SPICED PUMPKIN CREMEUX

400g pumpkin purée reduced to 200g, 30g egg yolks, 10g caster sugar, 10g custard powder, 3g gelatine, 125g butter, 1g ground star anise, 2g ground cinnamon, 2g ground mixed spice

Reduce the purée to 200g with the spices. Whisk the yolks, sugar and custard powder. Pour the purée over the egg mix and return to the pan, whisk constantly until boiling. Add the bloomed gelatine and stir well. Place the mix in a Thermomix, add the butter and blend on a low speed until emulsified. Bag and refrigerate ready for use.

Strawberry Lime Macarons

MACARON

1 batch basic macaron mix, 2g strawberry colour, 10g lime zest

Make the basic mixture as per the recipe, adding the lime zest to the almond base before adding meringue. Add the colouring to the meringue before mixing with almond base, then pipe and bake as instructed.

STRAWBERRY LIME BUTTERCREAM

140g caster sugar, 60g glucose, 40g water, 50g egg whites, 200g strawberry purée (reduced to 100g), 200g unsalted butter, 10g lime juice

Make an Italian meringue with the whites, sugar, water and glucose. Cook the sugar syrup to 121°C. Once the meringue is cold and stiff peaked, slowly add the softened butter on a low speed. Once the butter is incorporated add the reduced purée and the lime juice. Bag and refrigerate ready for use. When needed, pipe the buttercream to fill the macarons.

Golden Passion Macarons

MACARON

1 batch basic macaron mix, 5g yellow colour, 10g gold shimmer powder

Make the basic mixture as per the recipe, adding the gold shimmer powder to the almond base before adding meringue. Add the colouring to the meringue before mixing with almond base, then pipe and bake as instructed.

PASSIONFRUIT BUTTERCREAM

140g caster sugar, 60g glucose, 40g water, 50g egg whites, 80g passionfruit purée, 20g yoghurt crispies

Make an Italian meringue with the whites, sugar, water and glucose. Cook the sugar syrup to 121°C. Once the meringue is cold and stiff peaked, slowly add the softened butter on a low speed. Once the butter is incorporated add the purée. When needed, pipe the buttercream onto half of the macarons, sprinkle with some yoghurt crispies and then sandwich with another macaron.

Marshmallows

108 Small Sweets

Small Sweets 109

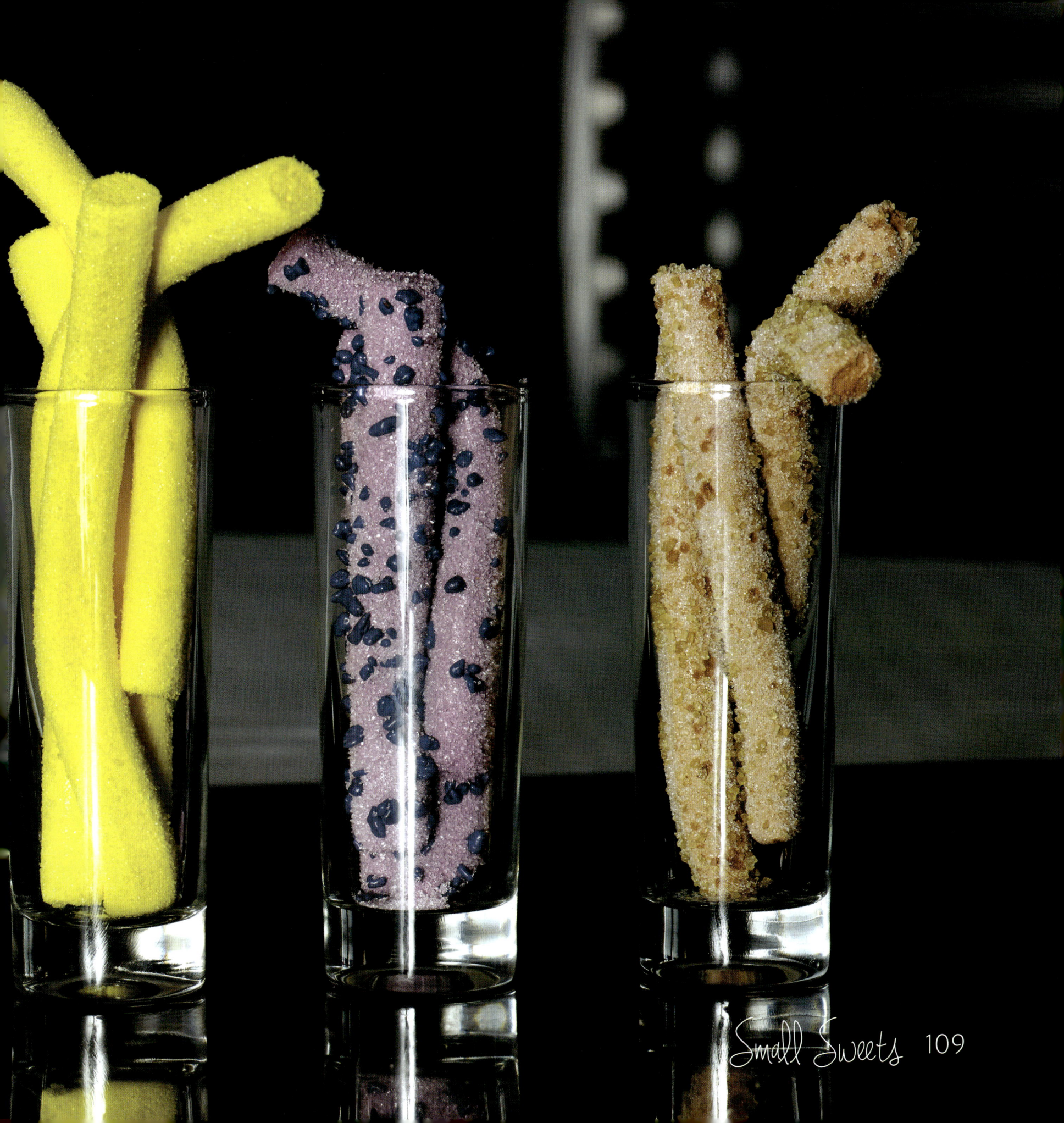

VARIATIONS:

Bubble Gum Marshmallow

300g caster sugar, 120g glucose, 60g water, 9.6g gelatine, 105g egg whites, 1g raspberry colour, 2g bubblegum essence, 10g hundreds and thousands

Make an Italian meringue with the sugar, water, glucose and egg whites. Once the sugar syrup is at 121°C add the bloomed gelatine and stir well, gradually pour over the egg whites. Whisk to a stiff meringue. Once cool, add the colour and essence. Pipe into lines on an acetate sheet. Sprinkle with hundreds and thousands. Leave for 8 hours to dry.

Cola Marshmallow

300g caster sugar, 120g glucose, 60g water, 9.6g gelatine, 105g egg whites, 2g citric acid, 1g demerara sugar , 2g caster sugar, 2g cola essence

Make an Italian meringue with the sugar, water, glucose and egg whites. Once the sugar syrup is at 121°C add the bloomed gelatine and stir well, gradually pour over the egg whites. Whisk to a stiff meringue. Once cool, add the colour and essence. Pipe into lines on an Acetate sheet. Sprinkle with the citric acid, and both sugars. Leave to dry for 8 hours.

Parma Violet Marshmallow

300g caster sugar, 120g glucose, 60g water, 9.6g gelatine, 105g egg whites, 4g crystallised violets, 2g violet colour.

Make an Italian meringue with the sugar, water, glucose and egg whites. Once the sugar syrup is at 121°C add the bloomed gelatine and stir well, gradually pour over the egg whites. Whisk to a stiff meringue. Once cool, add the colour. Pipe into lines on an acetate sheet. Sprinkle with crystallised violets. Leave to dry for 8 hours.

Popcorn Marshmallow

300g caster sugar, 120g glucose, 60g water, 9.6g gelatine, 105g egg whites, 3g popcorn essence , 2g yellow colour.

Make an Italian meringue with the sugar, water, glucose and egg whites. Once the sugar syrup is at 121°C add the bloomed gelatine and stir well, gradually pour over the egg whites. Whisk to a stiff meringue. Once cool, add the colour and essence. Pipe into lines on an acetate sheet. Leave to dry for 8 hours.

Small Sweets

Chocolate Madelines

75g caster sugar, 85g whole eggs, 1 Bourbon vanilla pod, 90g melted butter, 20g honey, 2g baking powder, 30g ground almonds, 50g T55 soft flour, 10g cocoa powder

Whisk the whole eggs and sugar in a mixer, adding the sugar in two stages, until a cold stiff sabayon is formed. Melt the honey and butter together. Sieve the almonds, flour and baking powder. On a low speed, add the vanilla seeds to the sabayon, followed by the dry ingredients, Finally, pour in the honey butter mix. Pour the mixture into tins and refrigerate for 1 hour before baking at 180°C for 6 minutes.

Lemon Honey Madelines

75g caster sugar, 85g whole eggs, 1 bourbon vanilla pod, 90g melted butter, 20g honey, 2g baking powder, 30g ground almonds, 60g T55 soft flour, 8g lemon zest

Whisk together the whole eggs and sugar, adding the sugar in two stages, until a cold stiff sabayon is formed. Melt together the honey, butter and lemon zest. Sieve the almonds, flour and baking powder. Add the vanilla pod seeds to the sabayon, followed by the dry ingredients on a low speed. Finally pour in the honey butter mix. Refrigerate the mix for 1 hour before baking. Bake the Madelines at 180°C for 6 minutes.

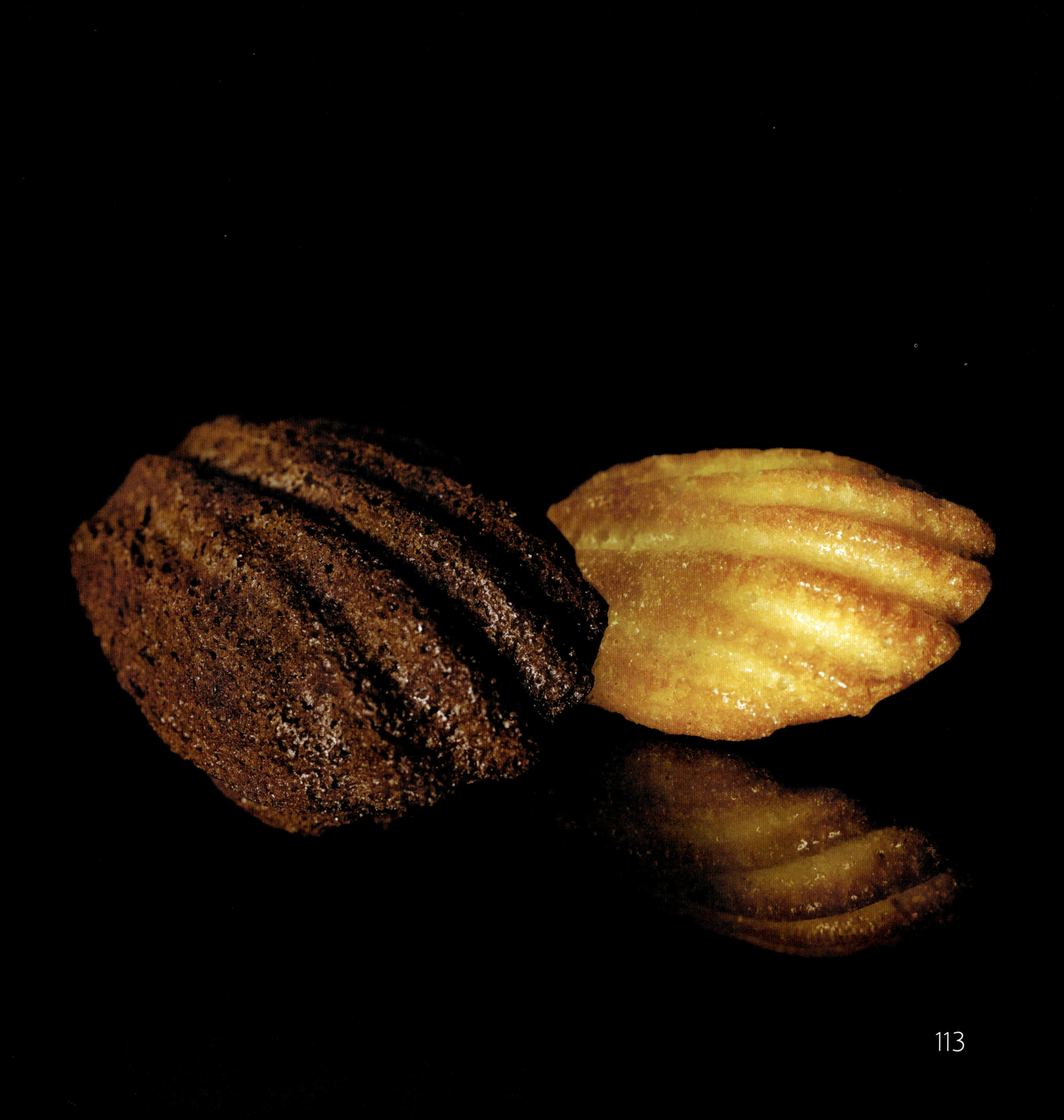

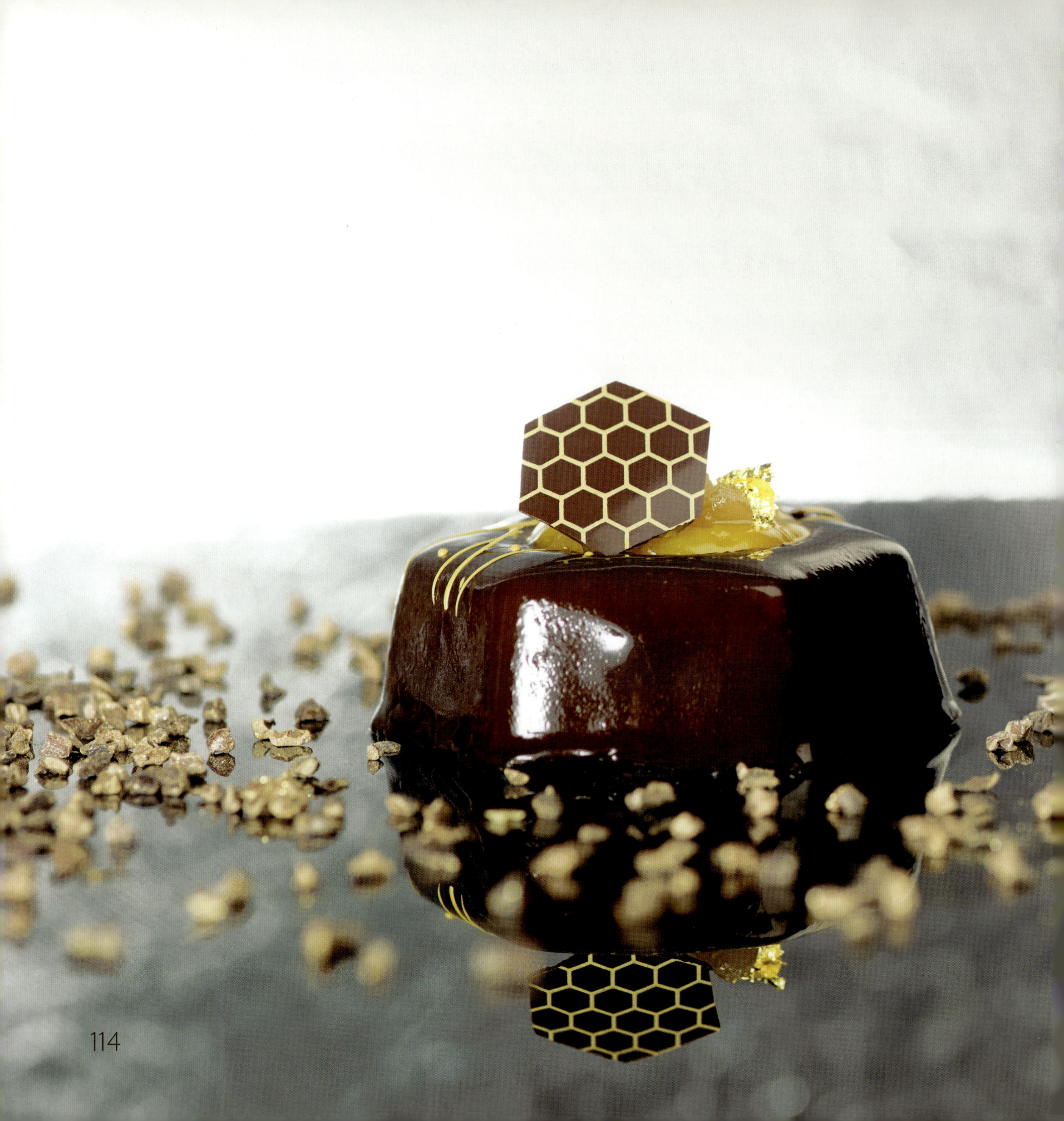

Petit Gateaux

Chocolate Mandarin Hazelnut

CHOCOLATE SABLEE BRETON

100g unsalted butter, 90g caster sugar, 1g fine salt, 45g egg yolks, 124g T55 soft flour, 6g coco powder, 4g baking powder

Cream the butter and sugar on a mixing machine with the paddle attachment. Add the egg yolks and the salt and mix to a smooth paste. Sieve the cocoa powder, flour and baking powder. Turn the machine down on a low speed and add the dry ingredients in two stages. As soon as the mix becomes a dough remove from the machine. Cling film the paste and refrigerate for one hour. Roll between two silicone sheets of paper and roll to 1cm depth. Bake at 165°C for 10 minutes cut when warm at 10cm by 3cm.

MANDARIN PATE D FRUIT

200g Mandarin purée, 80g caster sugar, 5.5g yellow pectin, 30g glucose, 2g orange zest, 2g citric acid, 1g water

Bring the glucose, purée and orange zest to the boil. Mix the sugar and pectin together. Gradually add the pectin sugar to the liquid, cook to 105°C. Add the citric acid and water and pour into mould to set. Cut 10cm by 3cm.

CHOCOLATE PAVE

62g Coeur De Guanaja 80% dark chocolate, 78g cocoa powder, 120g unsalted butter, 64g egg yolks, 10g whole egg, 60g caster sugar, 40g water, 180g whippped cream, 100g chopped caramelised hazelnuts

Make a pâte à bombe with the whole eggs, yolks, sugar and water. Whip the cream to ribbon stage. Melt the chocolate to 45°C, melt the butter to 40°C then mix to the two together. Sieve the cocoa powder, add to the chocolate butter mix, fold in the pâte à bombe, finally add the whipped cream. Pipe into mould to set.

HAZELNUT MOUSSE

70g egg yolks, 80g caster sugar, 20g water, 65g Tanariva milk chocolate, 180g whipping cream, 55g hazelnut paste

Make a pâte à bombe with the yolks, sugar and water, melt the Tanariva chocolate to 40°C. Whip the cream to ribbon stage. Add the hazelnut paste to the pâte à bombe, fold this mix into the melted chocolate. Finally fold in the whipped cream. Pipe into mould to set.

HAZELNUT PASTE

200g roasted hazelnuts, 20g hazelnut oil

Roast the hazelnuts at 175°C for 8 minutes until golden brown. Place the nuts and oil into a Thermomix and blend to a paste. Bag ready to use.

Pumpkin, Apple And Ginger Bread

GINGERBREAD BISCUIT

112g T55 soft flour, 2.4g bicarbonate of soda, 8g ground ginger, 3g ground cinnamon, 3g ground mixed spice, 53g unsalted butter, 53g black treacle, 52g golden syrup, 52g demerara sugar, 170g whole milk, 250g whole eggs

Bring the milk, spices, golden syrup, treacle and demerara sugar to the boil. Once boiling add the bicarbonate of soda and cook for 2 minutes on a medium heat, leave aside to cool. Cream the butter with a paddle attachment on a mixing bowl, add the whisked eggs and mix to a smooth paste. Add the spiced milk and finally the flour, mix until smooth. Leave the mix refrigerated overnight. The next day, pipe into a greased loaf tin and bake at 155°C for 30 minutes, then bake at 165°C for a further 15 minutes. Once cold slice and cut a small disc.

APPLE MOUSSE

125g Bramley apple juice, 125g apple purée, 45g egg yolks, 18g caster sugar, 5g water, 10g egg whites, 1g citric acid, 7g gelatine, 250g whipping cream

Bring the apple juice and purée to the boil, whisk the yolks. Pour the purée over the yolks and return to the heat, cook to 75°C. Add the bloomed gelatine and citric acid and stir well. Cool base to 25°C, whip the cream to ribbon stage. Make an Italian meringue and fold through the base, finally fold in the whipped cream, pipe into mould to set.

FENNEL BRULEE INSERT

155g whipping cream, 30g caster sugar, 25g whole eggs, 30g egg yolks, 2g fennel seeds, 2.3g gelatine

Roast the fennel seeds in a pan on a dry heat, add the cream and bring to the boil. Remove from the heat and cling film the pan, leave to infuse for 30 minutes. Whisk the whole eggs, yolks and sugar, bring the cream back to the boil and pour over the egg mix. Pass through a fine chinois and place in a tray. Bake at 90°C for 20 minutes until set. Once cooked place the brulee mix into a bowl and add the bloomed gelatine, stir well and chill the mix. Once cold, pipe into moulds to set.

PUMPKIN MOUSSE

120g pumpkin purée, 1g Ultratex, 0.5g fine salt, 26g egg yolks, 3g gelatine, 10g egg whites, 18g caster sugar, 120g whipping cream

Reduce the purée to 65g, once reduced add the Ultratex and salt. Whisk the yolks, pour the purée over the yolk and return to the heat. Cook to 75°C. Add the bloomed gelatine and stir well. Chill base to 25°C. Make an Italian meringue with the egg whites and caster sugar and fold into the base. Whisk the cream to ribbon stage and finally fold into the mix.

PUMPKIN SPRAY GEL

120g pumpkin purée, 1g Ultatex, 95g neutral glaze, fine salt, 3g gelatine

Reduce the pumpkin purée to 80g, add the Ultratex, salt and neutral glaze and bring to the boil. Add the bloomed gelatine and stir well. Chill the glaze. Place in spray gun and use at 32°C.

Peanut Butter Cherry Jam Doughnut

PEANUT BUTTER MOUSSE

40g caster sugar, 28g egg yolks, 2.1g gelatine, 15g water, 120g crunchy peanut butter, 80g peanut paste, 180g whipping cream

Make a pâte à bombe with the sugar, water and egg yolks, once the sugar syrup is 121°C, add the bloomed gelatine and stir well, gradually add to the egg yolks and whisk to cool. Separately, whisk the cream to ribbon stage. Warm the peanut paste and crunchy peanut butter to 30°C. Fold the pâte à bombe into the peanut mix, and finally fold in the cream. Pipe into the moulds to set.

DOUGHNUT GLAZE

160g caster sugar, 2g fine salt, 120g whole milk, 95g whipping cream, 10g gelatine, 60g drinking chocolate

Make a direct caramel with the sugar, adding it in 3 stages until a clear, golden brown. In a separate pan, bring the whole milk, whipping cream and salt to the boil. Add the cream milk mix in 4 stages to the caramel, emulsifying the caramel each time the liquid is added. Bring this mix back to the boil. Once boiling add the drinking chocolate and boil again. Add the bloomed gelatine. Pass the liquid through a muslin cloth. Chill the glaze, use at 25°C.

CHERRY JAM

200g sour cherry purée, 7g Ultratex, 1g citric acid

Hand blend all of the ingredients together until smooth, bag ready to use.

CHOCOLATE CHERRY BISCUIT

55g T55 soft flour, 5g cocoa powder, 10g cherry powder, 1.7g bicarbonate of soda, 55g unsalted butter, 43g Billingtons sugar, 19g caster sugar, 1.2g fine salt

Cream the butter and both sugars to a smooth paste. Sieve all the dry ingredients together. Add the cherry powder, cocoa powder and salt, followed by the flour and bicarbonate of soda. Mix to a smooth dough. Cling film the dough and refrigerate for one hour. Roll the dough to 1cm depth and bake at 170°C for 8 minutes. Cut as required.

Petit Gateaux 121

Raspberry Lychee Rose

RASPBERRY ROSE CREMEUX

200g raspberry purée, 30g egg yolks, 50g caster sugar, 12g custard powder, 3g gelatine, 125g butter, 1g rose essence

Bring the purée to the boil, whisk the yolks, sugar and custard powder together. Pour the purée over the egg mix and return to the heat, whisking constantly until the mix boils again. Remove from the heat and add the bloomed gelatine, stir well. Pour the mix into a Thermomix and on a low speed add the Rose essence and butter mix until emulsified. Bag ready to use.

LYCHEE MOUSSE

300g lychee purée, 20g egg yolks, 4.5g gelatine, 15g egg whites, 25g caster sugar, 110g whipped cream

Reduce the purée to 150g, whisk the egg yolks. Pour the purée over the yolk mix and cook to 75°C stirring constantly. Add the bloomed gelatine and chill the base to 25°C. Make an Italian meringue with the egg whites and caster sugar, fold this into the chilled base. Whip the cream to ribbon stage and fold in last. Pipe into mould to set.

LYCHEE INSERT

100g lychee jam, 50g raspberry purée, 30g diced fresh lychees, 3g raspberry crispies

Diced the fresh lychee into 0.5cm cubes and drain well. Mix with the lychee jam, raspberry purée and finally the crispies..Pipe into insert mould and freeze.

LYCHEE SPONGE

170g whole eggs, 240g caster sugar, 120g whipping cream, 225g T55 soft flour, 4g baking powder, 80g butter, 200g lychee jam

Whisk the whole eggs and caster sugar to a thick sabayon, gradually adding the sugar in 3 stages. Once a thick sabayon, pour in the whipping cream. Sieve the flour and the baking powder and fold into the mix. Finally add the melted butter. Spread onto a silicone mat and bake at 170°C for 12 minutes. Soak with the lychee jam once baked.

CRYSTALLISED ROSES

15g egg whites, 7g gum Arabic, 2g rose essence, 1 rose head, 10g caster sugar

Pick the rose head and remove the stem, lay the rose petals out. Mix the gum Arabic with the essence and egg whites. Brush each rose petal on each side with the egg mix, sprinkle with caster sugar. Leave at room temperature to crystalise for 12 hours

Petit Gateaux

Chocolate Passion Ginger

OLIVE OIL BISCUIT

90g unsalted butter, 80g Billingtons sugar, 140g T55 soft flour, 2.4g fine salt, 1 Tahiti vanilla pod, 1.2g baking powder, 36g egg yolks, 30g extra virgin olive oil

Cream the butter and sugar to a smooth paste in a mixing machine, with the paddle attachment. Add the yolks, olive oil, vanilla pod and salt and mix again. Sieve the flour and baking powder. Add the flour and baking powder in three stages until a soft dough is formed. Cling film the dough and refrigerate for 2 hours. Once rested, roll to 1.5cm depth and bake at 180°C for 8 minutes. Cut into 9cm by 2.5cm pieces.

CHOCOLATE PASSIONFRUIT CREAM

60g Andoa 70% dark chocolate, 30g caster sugar, 10g whole eggs, 15g egg yolks, 2.5g gelatine, 40g passionfruit purée, 70g whipping cream

Make a pâte à bombe with the whole eggs, yolks and caster sugar. Bring the purée to the boil, remove from the heat and add the bloomed gelatine. Melt the chocolate to 40°C. Whip the cream to soft peak stage. Pour the purée into the pâte à bombe, the. Fold this mix into the melted chocolate and stir well. Finally fold in the whipped cream and pipe into the mould to set.

CHOCOLATE GINGER MOUSSE

85g Tanariva 33% milk chocolate, 20g egg yolks, 5g caster sugar, 85g whipping cream, 2.5g gelatine, 70g whipped cream, 15g stem ginger paste

Blend the stem ginger to a paste. Melt the chocolate to 40°C. Make an anglaise with the cream, yolks, sugar and stem ginger, cook mix to 75°C. Remove from the heat, add the bloomed gelatine and stir well. Pour mix through a fine chinois over the meted chocolate. Chill base to 30°C. Whip the cream to soft peak stage and fold through the base, pipe into moulds to set.

PASSIONFRUIT GINGER FLUID GEL

50g orange juice, 50g passionfruit purée, 5g stem ginger paste, 1.5g agar agar, 15g caster sugar

Bring the orange juice, passionfruit purée and stem ginger paste to the boil., Mix the caster sugar and agar agar well, gradually add to the liquid and, whisking constantly bring back to the boil. Once boiling, pour onto a silicone mat and leave to set. Place in a Thermomix and blend to a smooth paste. Bag ready for use.

BITTER CHOCOLATE GLAZE

68g caster sugar, 120g water, 0.4g salt, 50g coco powder, 15g Coeur de Guanaja 80%, 100g neutral glaze, 1.4g gelatine

Bring the sugar, water, salt and coco powder to the boil. Add the chocolate and the glaze and boil again, whisking well. Add the bloomed gelatine and stir. Pass through a fine chinois and chill the glaze. Use at 28°C.

Rhubarb Custard Crumble Sphere

126 Petit Gateaux

RHUBARB BAVAROIS

125g rhubarb juice, 125g rhubarb jam, 35g egg yolks, 6g gelatine, 15g egg whites, 25g caster sugar, 5g water, 220g whipping cream

Bring the rhubarb juice and the purée to the boil. Whisk the egg yolks, pour the purée mix over the yolks and return to the heat. Cook the mix to 75°C stirring constantly. Add the bloomed gelatine. Chill this base to 25°C. Make an Italian meringue with the whites and sugar. Whip the cream to ribbon stage. Fold the meringue into the base, then finally fold in the whipped cream. Pipe into moulds to set.

RHUBARB JAM INSERT

100g rhubarb jam, 50g fresh rhubarb, 8g Grenadine

To poach the rhubarb, cut into 10cm batons, place in a tray and pour over the Grenadine. Cover with aluminium foil and cook in the oven at 180°C for 15 minutes. Once cold cut into 0.5cm dice. Mix with the rhubarb jam and pipe into moulds.

VANILLA CUSTARD INSERT

75g whole milk, 25g whipping cream, 20g egg yolks, 15g caster sugar, 1 Bourbon vanilla pod

Make an anglaise with all of the ingredients, cook to 75°C. Pass through a fine chinois and chill the mix. Once cold pipe onto insert mats.

LINZER PASTE

150g T55 soft flour, 90g unsalted butter, 50g ground brown almonds, 2g ground cinnamon, 1.5g ground cloves, 2g lemon zest, 50g caster sugar, 20g whole eggs, 10g egg yolks

Crumb all of the dry ingredients together with the butter, in a mixing machine with the paddle attachment. Add the whole eggs and yolks and mix to a smooth paste. Cling film the paste and refrigerate for 1 hour. Roll the paste to 0.5cm depth bake at 175°C for 10 minutes. When cooled, cut a small disc for the bottom of the sphere mould.

RHUBARB SPRAY MIX

250g white chocolate, 110g cocoa butter, 20g red cocoa butter

Melt the chocolate to 40°C, melt the cocoa butters to 35°C. Mix all together and pass through a muslin cloth. Place in a spray gun and use at 35°C.

Coconut Banana Mango

COCONUT DACQUOISE

100g ground almonds, 100g dessicated coconut, 200g icing sugar, 250g egg whites, 75g caster sugar

Whisk the egg whites and caster sugar in a mixing machine, adding the sugar in 3 stages until the meringue is at stiff peak stage. Sieve the almonds, coconut and icing sugar. Fold through the dry ingredients in 2 stages. Spread onto a silicone mat and bake at 170°C for 12 minutes. Cut discs as required.

CARAMELISED BANANA INSERT

150g demerara sugar, 1 banana, 25g rum

Dice the banana into 1cm cubes. Make a direct caramel with the demerara sugar. When the caramel is dissolved and clear add the diced banana. Stir the banana until coated in the caramel, deglaze with the rum. Once cold pipe into insert moulds.

MANGO BAVAROIS

300g Alphonso mango purée, 60g egg yolks, 10g whole milk, 6g gelatine, 20g egg whites, 30g caster sugar, 200g whipping cream

Reduce the purée to 200g with the milk, whisk the egg yolks. Pour the purée over the yolks and return to the heat, cook to 75°C. Remove from the heat and add the bloomed gelatine and stir well. Chill base to 25°C. Make an Italian meringue and fold into the base. Finally, whip the cream to soft peak and fold in. Pipe into moulds to set.

COCONUT LIME MOUSSE

300g coconut purée, 10g Malibu, 1g lime zest, 5g lime juice, 6g gelatine, 40g egg yolks, 75g sugar, 15g water, 160g whipped cream

Reduce the purée to 190g with the Malibu, lime zest and juice. Make a pâte à bombe with the sugar, water and yolks, once the sugar syrup is 121°C add the bloomed gelatine and stir well, gradually add to the whisking yolks, whisk until cool. Whip the cream to soft peak. Fold the coconut reduction into the pâte à bombe. Finally fold through the whipped cream. Pipe into moulds to set.

MANGO VANILLA LIME GLAZE

240g Alphonso mango purée, 12g lime juice, 125g neutral glaze, 2 vanilla pods de-seeded, 10g gelatine

Bring the purée and lime juice to the boil with the vanilla and neutral glaze. Once boiling add the bloomed gelatine and stir well. Chill the glaze and use at 29°C.

BANANA AND MANGO CREMEUX

200g mango purée, 100g banana purée, 30g egg yolks, 5g sugar, 12g custard powder, 3g gelatine, 125g butter

Reduce the mango purée to 100g, add the banana purée and bring to the boil. Whisk the yolks, sugar and custard powder, pour the purée over the egg mix and whisk well. Return to the pan. Whisking constantly, bring the mix back to the boil. Remove from the heat and add the bloomed gelatine and stir well. Place the mix in a Thermomix. On a low speed add the butter and blend the mix until emulsified. Pipe into small domes and freeze. Place on top of the gateaux ready for glazing.

Strawberry Yoghurt Meringue Tart

VANILLA SHORTCRUST

210g unsalted butter, 190g soft flour, 25g starch, 70g icing sugar, 10g egg yolks, 3g salt, 1 vanilla pod

Cream the butter and icing sugar together in a mixing machine with the paddle attachment. Once softened add the egg yolks, vanilla pod seeds and salt and mix again until smooth. Sieve the flour and starch and gradually add in 2 stages to form a dough. Cling film and refrigerate for 1 hour. Roll the dough to 0.3cm depth and line the tart case with the dough. Blind bake at 170°C for 10 minutes, remove the beans and bake at 175°C for 5 more minutes until golden brown.

YOGHURT CREMEUX

100g Greek yoghurt, 150g whole milk, 30g egg yolks, 10g caster sugar, 6g custard powder, 4g yoghurt powder, 1g lemon Juice, 2g gelatine, 125g butter

Bring the milk to the boil, whisk the yolks, sugar and custard powder. Pour the milk over the egg mix and return to the heat, whisking constantly bring the mix back to the boil. Remove from the heat, add the bloomed gelatine and stir well. Place in a Thermomix. On a low speed add the soft butter and mix until emulsified. Add the lemon juice, Greek yoghurt and yoghurt powder and blend until smooth. Bag ready for use.

STRAWBERRY MOUSSE

250g strawberry purée, 60g egg yolks, 5g Gelatine, 20g egg whites, 30g caster sugar, 170g whipping cream

Reduce the purée to 200g, whisk the egg yolks, pour the purée over the egg yolks and whisk well. Return to the heat and cook stirring constantly to 75°C. Add the bloomed gelatine and whisk until dissolved. Chill this base to 25°C. Make an Italian meringue and fold into the base, whip the cream to ribbon stage and fold through last. Pipe into moulds to set. Cut disc as required.

WHIPPED YOGHURT JELLY

120g whole milk, 10g Greek yoghurt, 5g yoghurt powder, 10g caster sugar, 6g gelatine

Place a mixing machine bowl and whisk in the freezer 1 hour prior to use. Bring the milk, yoghurt and yoghurt powder to the boil with the sugar. Once boiling add the bloomed gelatine and stir well. Chill the mix on an ice bath until set. Once set remove the bowl and whisk from the freezer, add the jelly and whisk on a high speed until aerated and doubled in volume. Transfer to a tray lined with an acetate sheet. Spread to 1cm depth and smooth with a palette knife. Refrigerate to set, then cut into 1cm cubes.

STRAWBERRY SHIMMER GLAZE

125g strawberry purée, 0.1g strawberry colour, 64g neutral glaze, 3.8g gelatine, 1g silver shimmer, 0.3g water

Bring the purée, colour and neutral glaze to the boil. Once boiling add the bloomed gelatine, stir until dissolved. Pass through a muslin cloth and chill the glaze. Use at 24°C. For the shimmer, mix the sliver shimmer and whisk with the water. Drop onto the glaze and spread with a palette knife.

WHITE CHOCOLATE DECORATION

20g red cocoa butter, 100g Opalys white chocolate pistols, 10g white cocoa butter

Temper the red cocoa butter and, using a brush dipped in the cocoa butter, flick over an acetate sheet. Melt two thirds of the white chocolate to 45°C. Melt the white cocoa butter, add to the chocolate. Add a third of the pistols and bring down to 26°C, stirring well. Bring the chocolate back up to 29°C and spread a thin layer over the set cocoa butter flick. Once set cut into discs using cutters.

Apricot Lemon Verbena Lollipop

APRICOT INSERT

190g apricot purée, 10g caster sugar, 3g pectin NH, 100g fresh apricots (1cm dice)

Bring the purée to the boil. Mix the pectin and the sugar together. Gradually add this to the boiling purée, whisking until the mix is boiling. Pass through a fine chinois and chill the liquid, fold through the diced apricots. Pipe into insert mould and leave to set.

LEMON VERBENA MOUSSE

110g whipping cream, 60g whole milk, 10g fresh lemon verbena, 20g egg yolks, 40g caster sugar, 12g water, 8g gelatine, 150g whipping cream

Bring the whipping cream, milk and lemon verbena to the boil. Place in a Thermomix and blend on full speed for several minutes until the aroma has been released. Return the mix back to a pan. Bring back to the boil then remove from the heat. Add the bloomed gelatine, stirring until dissolved. Pass through a muslin cloth and chill the mix to 20°C. Make a pâte à bombe with the egg yolks, sugar and water and fold through the verbena mix. Whisk the 150g of whipping cream to ribbon stage and fold through the mix last. Pipe into lollipop moulds, adding the insert half way. Leave to set and then pipe the remaining mix. Freeze moulds for 3 hours before remoulding.

APRICOT DIPPING MIX

500g Opalys white chocolate, 250g cocoa butter, 15g orange cocoa butter

Melt the chocolate to 45°C. Melt the cocoa butter to 40°C, with the orange cocoa butter.
Mix everything together and pass through muslin cloth. Use at 30°C to dip the lollipops.

GREEN CHOCOLATE MIX

100g Opalys white chocolate, 20g green cocoa butter

Melt the chocolate and cocoa butter separately to 45°C. Mix together and temper. Use at 29°C. Place in a small piping bag slowly pipe lines over the top of the dipped lollipop. Leave to set.

Petit Gateaux   133

Chocolate Bars

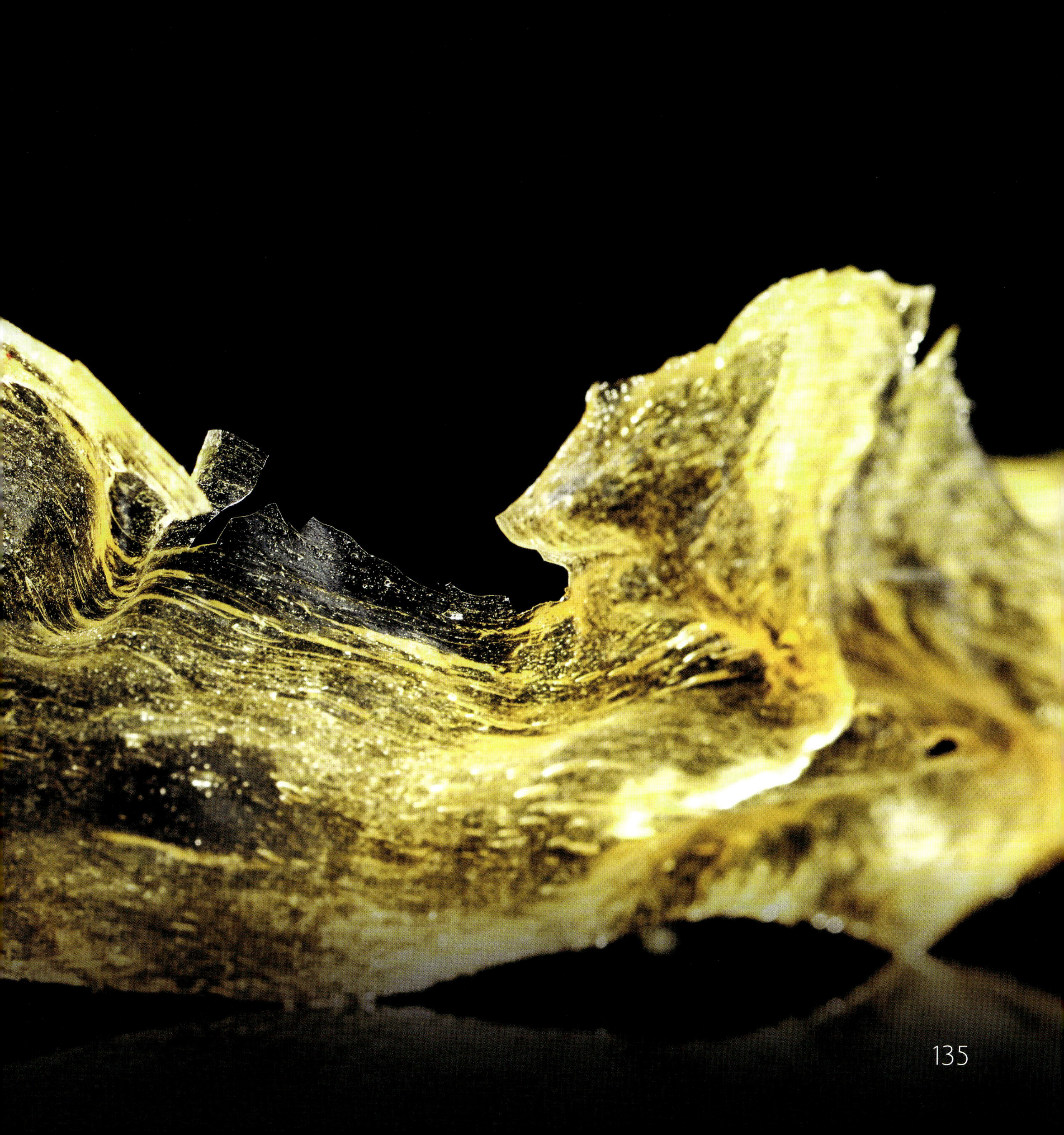

Snickers

SACHER

120g Guanaja 70% dark chocolate, 108g unsalted butter, 108g ground almonds, 64g egg yolks, 28g T55 soft flour, 96g egg whites, 108g caster sugar

Whisk the egg whites and sugar in a mixing machine, adding the sugar in 2 stages. Melt the chocolate to 40°C, melt the butter to 35°C, whisk together until emulsified. Add the egg yolk to the chocolate mix and whisk well. Whisk the meringue to a stiff peak, turn the machine down to a low speed and slowly pour in the chocolate mix, remove from the machine once a chocolate meringue is formed. Sieve together the ground almonds and flour. Pour into the chocolate meringue in 3 stages, mixing well with a scraper. Spread onto a silicone mat and bake at 165°C for 6 minutes. Once cold cut 2 rectangles 8cm by 2.5cm. Spread the bottom rectangles with a thin layer of tempered chocolate.

PEANUT PRALINE PASTE

150g salted peanuts, 280g castor sugar, 10g peanut oil

Roast the salted peanuts at 175°C for 8 minutes until golden brown. Make a direct caramel with the sugar adding, in several stages, until a clear golden brown. Add the roasted nuts and stir until all of the nuts are coated. Pour onto a silicone mat to cool and separate the nuts. Once cold, place in a Thermomix and blend to a paste with the oil. Bag ready to use. Use the paste to sandwich the sacher rectangles.

PEANUT GANACHE

120g peanut praline paste, 130g whipping cream, 250g Tanariva, 33% milk chocolate, 20g inverted sugar, 90g unsalted butter

Melt the chocolate to 40°C, add the inverted sugar and stir well. Bring the praline paste and cream to the boil, constantly stirring with a spatula. Pour the liquid over the chocolate in 3 stages and mix until smooth. Place in a Thermomix. On a low speed, gradually add the soft butter and blend until emulsified. Pipe into moulds to set.

CHOCOLATE SPRAY

200g Opayls white chocolate, 100g cocoa butter, 20g gold shimmer

Melt the chocolate to 45°C. Melt the cocoa butter to 40°C, add the gold shimmer and stir well. Mix with the chocolate and pass the liquid through muslin cloth. Use at 35°C to spray the ganache.

Jaffa Cake

ALMOND PAIN DE GENE

280g unsalted butter, 220g caster sugar, 280g ground almonds, 45g T55 soft flour, 45g cornflour, 250g whole eggs

Cream the butter and the sugar on a mixing machine with the paddle attachment, add half of the eggs and mix to a paste. Sieve the almonds the flour, add the dry ingredients in 2 stages. Add the remaining eggs and mix until smooth. Put the mix on a slicone mat and bake at 155c for 10 minutes then turn to 165°C for 5 minutes. Soak 200g syrup per sheet, cut rectangles at 8cm by 2.5cm x 3.

ORANGE VANILLA SYRUP

400g orange juice, 300g caster sugar, 10g orange zest, 4 Bourbon vanilla pods

Bring everything to the boil, cook to 48 Brix, use the syrup to soak the sponge.

ORANGE PATE D FRUIT

300g Mandarin purée, 3g orange zest, 80g caster sugar, 25g glucose, 5.5g yellow pectin, 2g citric acid, 1g water

Reduce the purée to 160g, add the zest and glucose and bring to the boil. Mix the sugar and pectin together and add to the boiling liquid gradually. Cook to 105°C, then mix the citric acid with the water and add to the liquid. Pour into a silicone mat to set. Once cold and set, place into a Thermomix and blend to a smooth paste. Use 20g per layer on top of the pain de gene, do this twice.

CHOCOLATE ORANGE GANACHE

63g Mandarin purée, 62g whipping cream, 115g Ashanti 67% dark chocolate, 1g orange zest, 10g inverted sugar, 45g unsalted butter

Bring the cream and purée to the boil with the zest. Remove from the heat and cling film the pan and leave to infuse for 30 minutes. Melt the the chocolate to 40°C, add the inverted sugar. Bring the purée cream back to the boil, add to the chocolate in 3 stages, mixing until smooth. Place in a Thermomix. On a low speed, add the soft butter and blend to emulsify.

CHOCOLATE GLAZE

62g water, 70g caster sugar, 10g whole milk, 52g whipping cream, 6g gelatine, 23g cocoa powder

Bring the water, sugar, milk and whipping cream to the boil, add the cocoa powder and whisk well bring back to the boil again, remove from the heat and add the bloomed gelatine, stir well. Pass through muslin cloth and chill the glaze. Use at 29°C.

Chocolate Bars 139

Oreo Peppermint

OREO COOKIE DOUGH

60g caster sugar, 98g T55 soft flour, 32g cocoa powder, 0.7g bicarbonate of soda, 1g salt, 86g unsalted butter

Cut the butter into small cubes. Place all the ingredients together in a mixing machine and with the paddle attachment work everything together to a dough. Cling film the dough and refrigerate for 1 hour. Roll to 1.5cm depth and bake at 170°C for 12 minutes. Cut as required.

PEPPERMINT BUTTERCREAM

140g caster sugar, 5g glucose, 30g water, 50g egg whites, 200g unsalted butter, 3g peppermint essence, 1g pistachio green colour

Make an Italian meringue with the sugar, water, glucose and egg whites, whisk to a stiff meringue. Add the softened butter. Once incorporated, add the essence and colour. Pipe onto half of the Oreo biscuits and sandwich together with the other half. Bring the cream to the boil, add the essence and leave aside. Melt the chocolate to 40°C, add the inverted sugar, add the cream in 3 stages, mix until smooth. Place in a Thermomix. On a low speed, add the soft butter and blend until emulsified. Pipe into mould to set.

CHOCOLATE PEPPERMINT GANACHE

125g whipping cream, 120g Araguani chocolate, 15g inverted sugar, 45g butter, 6g peppermint essence

Bring the cream to the boil, add the essence and leave aside. Melt the chocolate to 40°C, add the inverted sugar, add the cream in 3 stages, mix until smooth. Place in a Thermomix. On a low speed, add the soft butter and blend until emulsified. Pipe into mould to set.

Chocolate Bars 141

Bounty

COCONUT MERINGUE SPONGE

20g ground almonds, 60g desiccated coconut, 90g icing sugar, 100g egg whites, 30g caster sugar

Whisk the whites and the sugar on a mixing machine adding the sugar in 2 stages, whisk until a stiff meringue. Sieve the icing sugar and almonds, gradually fold through the coconut followed by the almonds and icing sugar, mix well with a scraper. Place the mix on a silicone tray bake at 170°C for 15 minutes. Soak with the coconut jam. Cut 8cm by 2.5cm.

TOASTED COCONUT GANACHE

300g coconut milk, 10g toasted desiccated coconut, 125g Tanariva 33% milk chocolate, 15g inverted sugar, 45g unsalted butter

Reduce the coconut milk to 150g. Melt the chocolate to 40°C add the inverted sugar to the chocolate and stir. Add the reduced milk in 3 stages to the chocolate mix, until smooth and glossy. Blend the chocolate with a hand blender, gradually adding the soft butter until the ganache is emulsified. Place in a bowl and fold through the toasted desiccated coconut. Pipe into mould to set.

COCONUT MILK JAM

200g coconut milk, 1g agar agar, 10g caster sugar

Reduce the coconut milk to 100g, mix the agar agar and sugar together, gradually pour this into the milk and bring back to the boil whisking constantly. Pour onto a silicone mat to cool. Once cold place into a Thermomix and blend to a smooth paste. Bag ready for use.

COCONUT MOUSSE

125g coconut milk, 10g Malibu, 30g egg yolks, 4g gelatine, 120g whipped cream, 5g toasted desiccated coconut

Bring the Malibu and purée to the boil. Whisk the egg yolks. Pour the purée over the yolks and return to the heat, cook to 75°C stirring constantly. Remove from the heat and add the bloomed gelatine. Chill base to 25°C. Whisk the cream to soft peak and fold into the base. Finally add the toasted desiccated coconut and pipe into mould to set.

MILK SPRAY MIX

200g Jivaria 40% milk chocolate, 100g coconut butter, 20g bronze shimmer

Melt the chocolate to 40°C, melt the cocoa butter to 35°C. Mix together and add the gold shimmer. Pass through muslin cloth and place in a spray gun. Use at 35°C.

Raspberry Wagon Wheel

VANILLA SHORTBREAD

200g unsalted butter, 100g caster sugar, 150g ground almonds, 20g egg yolks, 150g T55 soft flour

Cream the butter and the sugar on a mixing machine with the paddle attachment. Add the egg yolks and mix to a smooth paste. Sieve the almonds and flour and fold into the mix in 2 stages. Once a dough is formed, cling film and refrigerate for 1 hour. Roll out the dough to 1.5cm depth and bake at 170°C for 9 minutes. Cut disc as required.

RASPBERRY JAM

250g raspberries, 50g jam sugar, 1g citric acid

Place all the ingredients in a pan and cook on a medium heat to 62 Brix with a refractometer. Chill ready for use.

VANILLA MARSHMALLOW

150g caster sugar, 60g glucose, 30g water, 2 Tahiti vanilla pods, 52g egg whites, 4.8g gelatine

Cook the sugar, glucose and water to 121°C, add the bloomed gelatine to the sugar syrup and stir well. Gradually pour over the whisking egg whites, add the vanilla seeds and whisk to a stiff meringue. Pipe into a dome on top of the jam and shortbread biscuit and leave 8 hours to dry.

DIPPING GLAZE

200g Caraibe 66% dark chocolate, 60g cocoa butter

Melt the chocolate to 40°C, melt the cocoa butter to 30°C. Mix together and pass through a muslin cloth. Use at 30°C to dip the marshmallow. Leave on a tray to crystallise and set.

Chocolate Bars 145

Caramel Popcorn Bar

146 *Chocolate Bars*

POPCORN MILK

30g cooked popcorn, 200g caster sugar, 1000g milk

Make a direct caramel with the sugar, gradually adding it in stages. Add the popcorn and coat evenly, add the milk and bring to the boil. Place in a Thermomix and blend on full speed for 10 minutes. Place in a vacuum pac bag and seal everything, leave to infuse for 24hrs before using.

POPCORN GANACHE

125g popcorn milk, 25g Greek yoghurt, 280g Biskella 34% milk chocolate, 50g caster sugar, 50g unsalted butter

Melt the chocolate to 40°C, Bring the popcorn milk to the boil. Make a direct caramel with the sugar and cook until a clear golden brown, deglaze with the popcorn milk. Add this liquid to the melted chocolate in 3 stages. Mix until smooth and glossy. With a hand blender, add the yoghurt and the butter and blend until smooth. Pipe into moulds to set.

CHOCOLATE SHORTPASTE

48g butter, 27g caster sugar, 100g T55 soft flour, 28g cocoa powder, 15g egg yolks, 1g salt

Sieve together the flour, cocoa powder and salt. Cream the butter and sugar until soft, in a mixing machine with a paddle attachment. Add the egg yolks and mix until a smooth paste. Add the dry ingredients in 2 stages until a smooth dough. Cling film the dough and refrigerate for 1 hour to firm. Roll out to 1cm depth and bake at 170°C for for 9 minutes. Cut 8cm by 2.5cm. Brush a thin layer of tempered chocolate on the bottom of the biscuit.

POPCORN MOUSSELINE

100g popcorn milk, 10g caster sugar, 20g egg yolks, 8g custard powder, 67g unsalted butter

Bring the popcorn milk to the bowl. Whisk the yolks, sugar and custard powder. Pour the boiling liquid over the egg mix and return to the heat, whisking constantly until the mix re boils.

Chill this mix to 5°C then place into a mixing machine with a whisk attachment. Add the softened butter, whisk until fully incorporated and smooth. Pipe into moulds to set.

Salted Caramel Almond Crunchy

SALTED CARAMEL CRUNCH

200g salted caramel sauce, 50g toasted nibbed almonds, 30g feuilletine, 50g Jivaria milk chocolate

Toast the nibbed almonds at 175°C for 8 minutes until golden brown. Melt the chocolate to 40°C, add the feuilletine, salted caramel sauce and almonds and mix well. Roll between two sheets of silicone paper to 1cm depth and leave to crystallise. Cut 8cm by 2.5cm.

SPICED GINGER BISCUIT

50g unsalted butter, 45g caster sugar, 0.5g fine salt, 25g egg yolks, 63g T55 soft flour, 1g ground ginger, 2g ground mixed spice, 1g ground cinnamon, 2g baking powder

Cream the butter and sugar in a mixing machine with the paddle attachment. Add the egg yolk and salt and mix to a smooth paste. Sieve all of the dry ingredients with the spices. Add the dry ingredients in 2 stages and mix to a smooth paste. Cling film and refrigerate for 1 hour. Roll out on a silicone sheet to 1cm depth and bake at 165°C for 12 minutes until golden brown.

CARAMELISED ALMOND PASTE

200g caster sugar, 100g toasted whole blanched almonds, 20g groundnut oil

Toast the almonds at 170°C for 10 minutes until golden brown. Make a direct caramel with the sugar until a clear caramel. Add the nuts and stir until fully coated in caramel. Pour onto a silicone mat and separate the nuts. Leave to cool. Blend in a Thermomix with the oil to a smooth paste. Bag ready to use.

CARAMEL ALMOND MOUSSE

50g caramelised almond paste, 30g Dulcey 32% milk chocolate, 100g caster sugar, 200g whole milk, 45g egg yolks, 6g gelatine, 0.5g fine salt, 240g whipped cream

Bring the milk to the boil with the salt, whisk the egg yolks. Pour the hot milk over the yolks and return to the heat, stirring constantly until the liquid thickens and reaches 75°C. Remove from the heat and add the bloomed gelatine. Melt the chocolate to 40°C, add the caramelised almond paste and the milk base and stir well. Chill this base to 30°C. Whip the cream to ribbon stage and fold into the chilled base. Pipe into moulds to set.

SPICED CARAMEL BAVAROIS

100g caster sugar, 2g star anise, 1 cinnamon stick, 1 cardamon pod, 125g whole milk, 125g whipping cream, 50g egg yolks, 10g egg whites, 18g caster sugar, 5g water, 3g gelatine, 210g whipping cream

Roast the spices in a pan on a dry heat until the aroma is released. Add the 100g of sugar in several stages until a clear caramel is formed. Deglaze with the milk and whipping cream and bring back to the boil. Whisk the yolks and pour the spiced caramel milk over the yolks. Return to the heat and stirring constantly cook this base to 75°C. Add the bloomed gelatine and stir well. Pass through a fine chiniois. Chill the base to 25°C. Make an Italian meringue with the 18g of sugar and egg whites and fold into the base. Whip the cream to ribbon stage and fold through the base last. Stir well with a spatula and pipe into moulds to set.

Banoffee Pie

BISCUIT BASE

100g toasted spiced ginger biscuit, 100g toasted vanilla Sablé Breton, 50g butter

Crush the toasted ginger biscuit and Sablé Breton to a biscuit crumb. Melt the butter to 25°C and pour into the biscuit mix, stir with a spatula and press into the mould. Refrigerate to set.

TOFFEE CARAMEL

100g caster sugar, 100g demerara sugar, 20g butter, 10g glucose, 200g whipping cream

Melt the caster sugar and demerara sugar in a pan until a dark brown caramel. Once fully melted, add the glucose and butter and stir well. Once dissolved, add the cream and bring to the boil. Reduce by half, leave to cool. When cold spread a layer on top of the set biscuit.

CARAMELISED BANANA MOUSSE

200g demerara sugar, 2 diced bananas, 30g rum, 40g egg yolks, 80g caster sugar, 15g water, 4g gelatine , 240g whipping cream

Place the demerara sugar in a pan and caramelise. Cut the banana to 1cm dice and add to the caramel, stir until fully coated, deglaze with the rum. Place in a jug and blitz with a hand blender until smooth. Make a pâte à bombe with the yolks, sugar and water, once the syrup is 121°C add the bloomed gelatine and stir well. Gradually pour this over the whisking yolks and then whisk until cool. Fold the pâte à bombe into the banana Purée. Whip the cream to soft peak and fold this in last. Pipe into mould to set.

VANILLA CREMEUX

200g whole milk, 3 Tahiti vanilla pods, 30g egg yolks, 20g caster sugar, 12g custard powder, 3g gelatine, 125g butter

Bring the milk, vanilla seeds and pods to the boil. Whisk the yolks, sugar and custard powder. Pour the boiling milk through a fine chinois over the egg mix. Return to the heat whisking constantly until the mix returns to the boil. Remove from the heat, add the bloomed gelatine and stir. With a hand blender, blend the mix adding the soft butter until emulsified.

BANANA GEL GLAZE

100g banana purée, 150g whipping cream, 125g clear neutral glaze, 90g caster sugar, 10g gelatine

Make a direct caramel with the sugar, once a clear golden brown, deglaze with the cream. Bring to the boil, add the banana purée and the glaze. Bring back to the boil. Add the bloomed gelatine, and stir well. Pass through a fine chinos once at the mix is at 29°C. Use to glaze the gateaux.

Chocolate Bars 151

Patisserie Perfection

INDEX OF RECIPES:

CHOCOLATES 10
BLACKCURRANT VIOLET 18
BURNT SUGAR 24
COCONUT LEMONGRASS 36
FRESH MINT 20
HIBISCUS 46
LAVENDER & HONEY 14
LEMON BASIL 30
LEMON THYME 22
MANDARIN ORANGE BLOSSOM 16
MANGO CARAMEL LIME 48
MATCHA 44
PASSIONFRUIT, GINGER SALT 38
RASPBERRY ROSE 40
SALTED PEANUT 26
SESAME 32
SPICED ANISE 28
TAHITI VANILLA 42
TONKA BEAN 34
WILD STRAWBERRY 12
DECONSTRUCTED DESSERTS 50
APPLE PIE AND CUSTARD 62
BLACK FOREST GATEAU 52
ETON MESS 59
LEMON MERINGUE PIE 60
PEACH MELBA 56
PINA COLADA RUM BABA 64
ENTREMETS 66
CHOCOLATE TONKA PRALINE 84
PEANUT CARAMEL AZTEC 88
PISTACHIO & APRICOT GATEAU 76
STRAWBERRIES & CREAM 72
TROPICAL 68
WOODLAND FOREST 80

SMALL SWEETS 92
APPLE CALVADOS PATE D' FRUIT 99
BLOOD ORANGE TURKISH DELIGHT 100
BUBBLE GUM MARSHMALLOW 110
CHOCOLATE MADELEINES 112
COLA MARSHMALLOW 110
GOLDEN PASSION MACARONS 107
JASMINE TEA MACARONS 106
LEMON HONEY MADELEINES 112
MARSHMALLOW 108
MINI MACARONS 102
MINT & LEMON MACARONS 105
NOUGAT DE MONTELIMAR 94
PARMA VIOLET MARSHMALLOW 111
POPCORN MARSHMALLOW 111
RASPBERRY SHERBET PATE D' FRUIT 98
SPICED GINGERBREAD MACARONS 104
SPICED PUMPKIN MACARONS 106
STRAWBERRY LIME MACARONS 107
YUZU & LIME PATE D' FRUIT 96
PETIT GATEAUX 58
APRICOTLEMONVERBENALOLLIPOP 132
COCONUT BANANA MANGO 128
CHOCOLATE MANDARIN HAZELNUT 116
CHOCOLATE PASSION GINGER 124
PEANUT BUTTER CHERRY JAM DOUGHNUT 120
PUMPKIN, APPLE AND GINGERBREAD 118
RASPBERRY LYCHEE ROSE 122
RHUBARB CUSTARD CRUMBLE SPHERE 126
STRAWBERRY YOGHURT MERINGUE TART 130
CHOCOLATE BARS 134
BANOFFEE PIE 148
BOUNTY 140
CARAMEL POPCORN BAR 144
JAFFA CAKE 138
OREO PEPPERMINT 141
RASPBERRY WAGON WHEEL 142
SALTED CARAMEL ALMOND CRUNCHY 146
SNICKERS 136

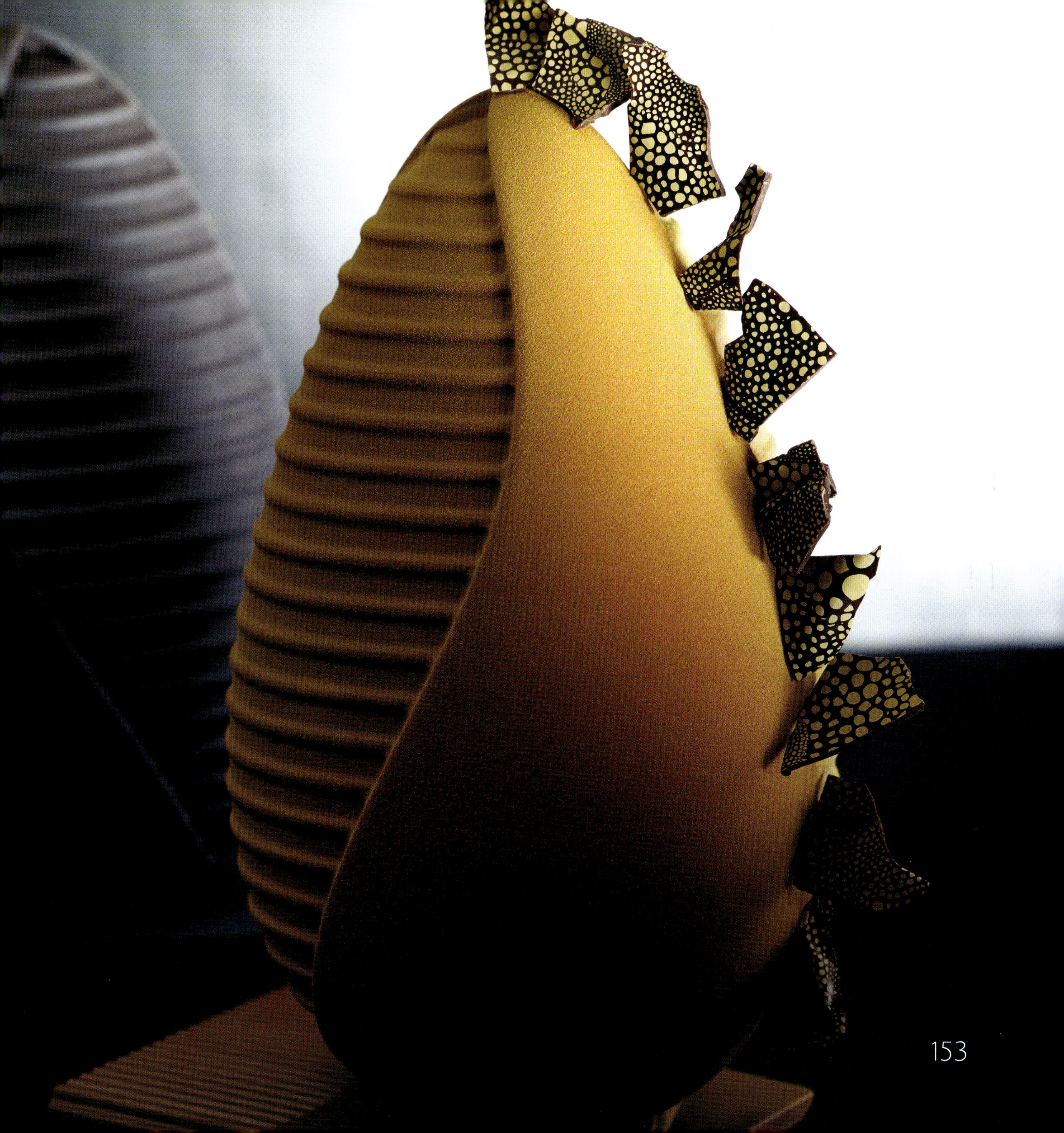

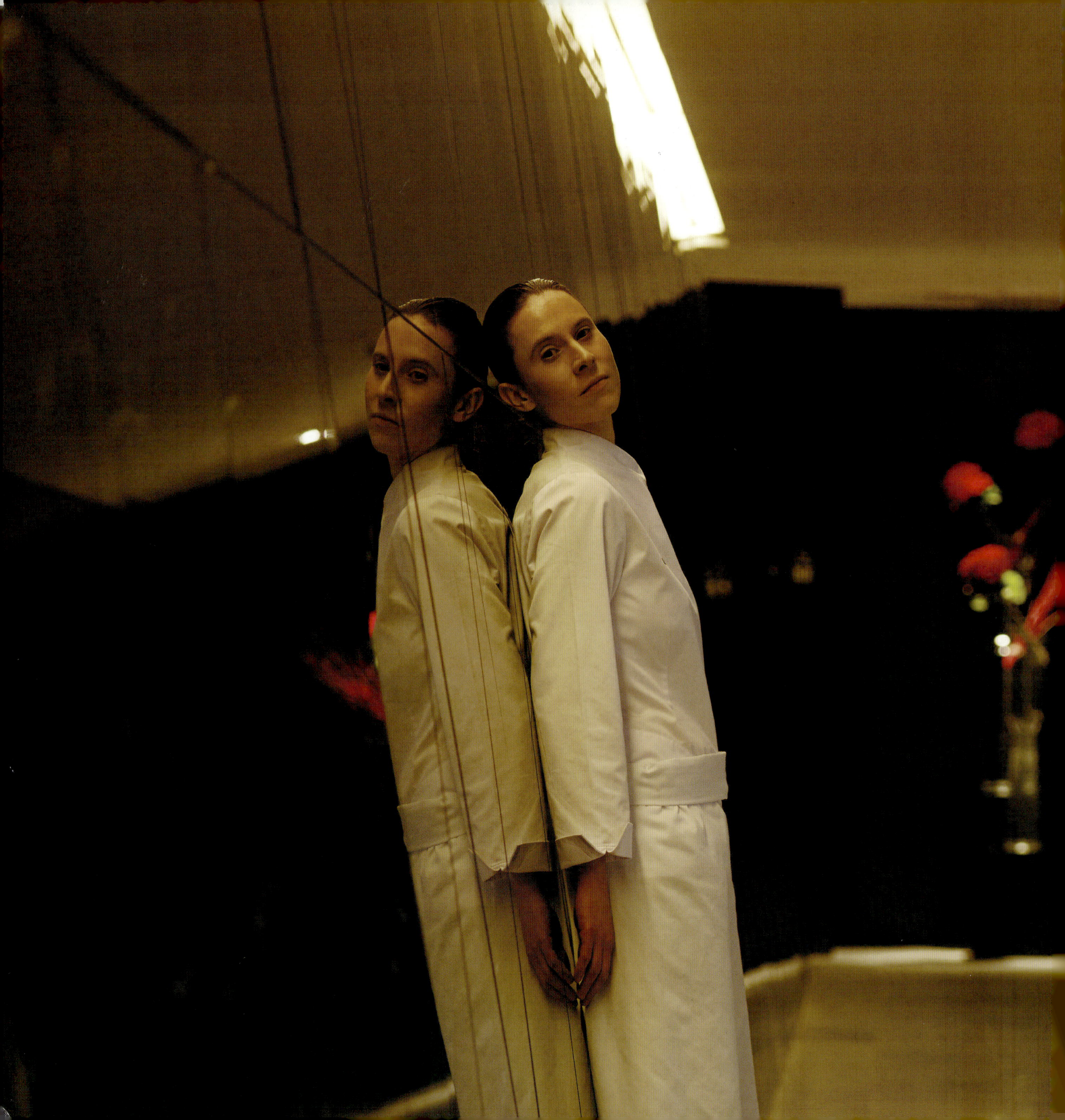

Sarah Barber
is patisserie perfection

ACKNOWLEDGEMENTS

I WOULD LIKE TO SAY A SPECIAL THANK YOU TO EVERYONE WHO WAS INVOLVED TO HELP ME CREATE THIS BOOK:

My Pastry team at ME London, for all their support and assistance during the project

To all the pastry chefs who have ever worked with me, for being on the journey so far, thank you for all your hard work.

And a special thank you to Peter Marshall who believed in me enough to publish this book and for his amazing photography

To the friends and companies who helped me with equipment and ingredients

OLIVER BATEL - Classic Fine Foods

DIANA CASCIO - Pavoni Italia

DOMINIQUE MULLER - PCB Creation

PAUL GOODFELLOW - Goodfellows

MICHAEL KAMLISH - Home Chocolate Factory

MARIE VAN BRANTEGHEM & ANDRE DANG - VALRHONA

JULIE SHARP - BARRY CALLEBAUT

ChefMEDIA

First published in 2015 by Chef Media Ltd

Copy write Peter Marshall

The rights of the author have been asserted. All rights reserved.

No part of this book may be reproduced, stored in a retrieval system or transmitted in any form or by any means electronic electrostatic, magnetic tape mechanical, photocopying recording or otherwise, without the prior permission in writing from the publisher.

ISBN 978-1-908202-21-5

Author Sarah Barber

Publisher Chef Media ltd

Editor Shirley Marshall

Designer Andrew Shugan, www.andrewshugan.ua,

Designer Olga Pomazkova, www.opdesign.com.ua

Photography Peter Marshall

www.chefmedia.co.uk